Market Town Wales

Written and photographed by **David Williams**.

GRAFFEG

Published by Graffeg
Copyright © Graffeg 2010
ISBN 978 1 905582 23 5

Graffeg, Radnor Court,
256 Cowbridge Road East,
Cardiff CF5 1GZ Wales, UK
T: +44 (0)29 2037 7312
sales@graffeg.com
www.graffeg.com

Market Town Wales is written and
photographed by David Williams,
words and pictures © copyright
David Williams 2010.

Designed and produced by
Peter Gill & Associates
sales@petergill.com
www.petergill.com

Distributed by the Welsh Books
Council www.cllc.org.uk
castellbrychan@cllc.org.uk

A CIP catalogue record for this book
is available from the British Library

Graffeg books are available from all
good bookshops and online from
www.graffeg.com

Other titles published by Graffeg:
• Landscape Wales
• Coastline Wales
• About Wales
• About South West Wales
• About South East Wakes
• About Mid Wales
• About North Wales
• Pocket Wales Landscape Wales
• Pocket Wales Coast Wales
• Pocket Wales Castles of Wales
• Pocket Wales Mountain Wales
• Welsh National Opera
• Food Wales – a second helping
• Food Wales eating out guide
• Bryan Webb's Kitchen: Tyddyn Llan
• Celtic Cuisine
• Golf Wales
• Village Wales
• Skomer Island
• Caldey Island
• Pembrokeshire
• Seashore Safaris
• Senedd
• Discovering Welsh Houses
• Discovering Welsh Gardens

The publisher acknowledges the
financial support of the Welsh
Books Council www.gwales.com

Market Town Wales

Written and photographed by **David Williams**.

GRAFFEG

Market days

The market towns in this book hold a wide range of produce markets, farmers' markets, craft and antiques fairs. We have listed market days for each town, but it is advisable to check days and times with the local Tourist Information Centre (TIC), or the web, if you're planning a visit.

Livestock market days

Livestock markets are not open to the general public for reasons of safety and animal health.

For information about attractions, events and accommodation throughout Wales, visit www.visitwales.co.uk and www.cadwevents.co.uk

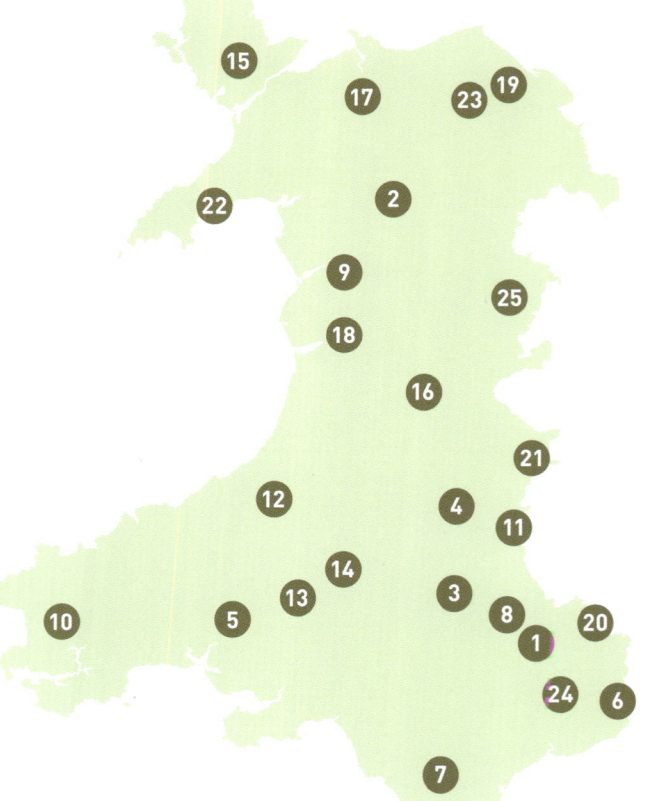

Contents

Introduction		6
1.	Abergavenny	8
2.	Bala	16
3.	Brecon	24
4.	Builth Wells	32
5.	Carmarthen	40
6.	Chepstow	48
7.	Cowbridge	58
8.	Crickhowell	66
9.	Dolgellau	76
10.	Haverfordwest	86
11.	Hay-on-Wye	92
12.	Lampeter	102
13.	Llandeilo	110
14.	Llandovery	118
15.	Llangefni	126
16.	Llanidloes	134
17.	Llanrwst	144
18.	Machynlleth	152
19.	Mold	162
20.	Monmouth	172
21.	Presteigne	182
22.	Pwllheli	190
23.	Ruthin	196
24.	Usk	206
25.	Welshpool	214
Index		222

Introduction

Market Town Wales explores places that grew to serve the communities and commerce of the countryside; places that have been central to the Welsh economy since medieval times.

The Romans understood that the town, and ultimately the city, was a good way of organising society. Their regional capitals – Venta Silurum (Caerwent) and Moridunum (Carmarthen) – held the record as Wales's largest towns for several centuries. In late-medieval times, and especially after the Industrial Revolution, larger centres of population began to grow. People from rural areas felt that they could better themselves by moving into the towns; indeed, they were essential to the workforce.

Look at a map of Wales and you will see perhaps fifty towns, their names in medium-sized lettering. Some occupy defensive sites and, in typical Welsh fashion, are overlooked by a castle. Others are seaports; the coastline provided sheltered harbours and access inland along river valleys. The linear towns of the southern coalfield, the quarry communities of Snowdonia and the industrial centres of north-east Wales attracted the thousands engaged in extracting and processing coal, slate and metal ores. In some fortunate places, the scenic attractions of mountains and coast, and the discovery of therapeutic springs, gave rise to holiday resorts and spa towns.

But it is the market towns that tend to have the longest histories, the most character and many of the most handsome buildings. The promotion from village to town was made by the granting of a municipal charter to hold a regular livestock market or fair.

This was a much-prized affirmation of the importance of a community in its ability to serve and sustain its rural hinterland.

Many livestock markets, and several fairs, continue today but the market towns have also acquired new attributes: produce markets, shops, restaurants, theatres, arts centres and museums. Their convenient locations, typically where valleys and roads meet, mean that their residents enjoy good communications and an appealing quality of life; they are sought-after places in which to live and work. Wales's largest towns, Wrexham, Newtown, Pontypridd and others, have become major centres of local government and education. The outstandingly good indoor markets in our largest cities such as Cardiff, Swansea and Newport, echo their earlier history as market centres.

This book explores twenty-five small to medium-sized country towns that encapsulate the image of a 'historic market town of character'. There is something about their eclectic mix of buildings, their self-sufficient provision of local services and their energetic daily bustle that feels just right. Choosing them was not always easy; there are often other attractive and historic towns nearby so be sure to seek them out!

The market towns of Wales are making strenuous efforts to preserve their character in the face of out-of-town and online shopping, and the relentless uniformity and blandness that has overwhelmed many a high street. They are precious national treasures and a joy to visit, we will get to know a pleasing selection of them in these pages.

David Williams.

Abergavenny

Abergavenny is well connected, by means of good roads, to the surrounding area. The Heads of the Valleys road (A465) passes just to the south of the town and continues northward to Hereford; the A4042 connects to the M4, some eighteen miles to the south; the A40 extends into mid Wales. The town also has a railway station. Abergavenny has a population of 9,628.

Market days
Tuesday, Friday and Saturday

The way in which geography determines the positions of market towns is very evident at Abergavenny. This is where the mountainous terrain of central Wales meets the fertile plains of Gwent, and the river Usk emerges from its narrow valley to meander through the lowlands of Monmouthshire to its estuary at Newport. Viewed from the lower slopes of the Sugar Loaf mountain, the town sits comfortably amid productive farming country. The castle, the verdigris-green roof of the Market Hall and the tower of St Mary's Priory Church stand above the town centre.

The Roman settlement here was a place where iron was produced and worked into tools and equipment. It was called Gobannium, of which the present name of the town is an echo – the river Gavenny flows into the Usk here at its aber, the Welsh for the mouth of a river. In another resonance with Rome, Abergavenny is set against a background of seven graceful mountains including The Sugar Loaf, The Skirrid and The Blorenge.

The castle grew on the site of a small Norman motte-and-bailey dating from around 1097. Here in 1182 William de Breos infamously murdered his dinner guests, the Welsh chieftain Seisyll ap Dyfnwal and his supporters, who had (as was the custom) politely left their swords at the door.

During Tudor times, Abergavenny outgrew its original fortified perimeter. It was a Royalist stronghold during the Civil War and, when threatened by Parliamentarian forces in 1645, the castle was destroyed to prevent its use by Cromwell's army. The wool trade, including the weaving of flannel, sustained the town during the seventeenth and eighteenth centuries. Leather tanning was also an important activity and the making of wigs from goat hair was a speciality.

During the Industrial Revolution, the booming population of the coal-mining and iron-producing valleys immediately to the south-west generated a healthy demand for produce from Abergavenny's markets. The arrival of the railway during the 1850s strengthened the town's position even more.

Today, Abergavenny is a popular shopping and cultural centre, and a good base from which to explore the delights of the Brecon Beacons and the Black Mountains. The surrounding region offers adventure activities including walking, cycling, climbing, gliding, paragliding, sailing and pony trekking. It is also an excellent centre for touring the region by car or public transport; Brecon, Monmouth, Hay-on-Wye and Hereford are all within twenty-five miles.

Abergavenny Market Hall is one of the busiest in Wales and is worth a visit at any time of year, for the wide range of foods, plants and household goods available from the friendly stallholders. Market days are Tuesday, Friday and Saturday; the attractions also include a Flea Market on Wednesdays, a Craft Fair on the second Saturday of each month and a Farmers' Market on the fourth Thursday of each month. The Market Hall is also the main venue for the Abergavenny Food Festival, held each year during mid-September.

Food is a recurring theme in Abergavenny, during the Food Festival and throughout the year – in the market, in the numerous food shops and in the high-quality cafés and restaurants.

Right: The Shire Horse Show, held during late July in Bailey Park is one of the most colourful occasions. The animals, their owners and the carts and farm equipment they demonstrate (and on which the rural economy once depended) are all immaculately turned out for the judges to inspect.

Opposite top left: Many of the town's fine buildings, including the former homes of merchants, have been put to new uses as business premises. However others, including long-established banks, remain in their original roles. There are some intriguing details; the sixteenth-century home of the Vaughan family in Nevill Street became the Cow Inn during the eighteenth century and is identified as such by the row of carved cows' heads under its eaves.

Opposite top right: There are numerous specialist shops (this is Xenia in Lewis's Lane) selling gifts and decorative items of great appeal, some made by craftsmen in Wales, others from overseas.

Opposite below: St Mary's Priory Church was established by Hamelin de Ballon, the Norman overlord of the region, in 1087 – as a cell of the Abbey of St Vincent near Le Mans, Normandy. It contains one of the UK's best collections of medieval tombs and memorials, commemorating local ruling families. The magnificently bearded figure of Jesse, father of King David, was carved from a single oak trunk and is a remarkable example of late-fifteenth century craftsmanship. Be sure also to visit the splendidly restored tithe barn nearby, where there is a fascinating exhibition about Abergavenny's history and a Food Hall serving locally sourced produce.

Above: Abergavenny Museum occupies a former hunting lodge built on the summit of the castle site in 1819. Its displays include this reconstruction of a typical Welsh farmhouse kitchen from around 1890, which hints at the daily lives of the people who depended upon the market towns for the sale of their produce. Life was tough and the hours were long and hard; farming was, as it remains today, a battle against both the elements and the landscape.

THOMAS CHARLES

1755 – 1814

Bala

Bala is eighteen miles north-east of Dolgellau, along the A494, and ten miles south-west of Corwen. It grew where the river Dee flows out of Bala Lake. Bala has a population of 1,980.

Market day
Monday

The Anglican clergyman Thomas Charles, originally from Carmarthenshire, married Sally Jones of Bala and settled locally. Finding that the new Methodist ideas chimed with his own, he joined the congregation here in 1784 and became a minister, writer and publisher. Thanks to his talents and ideas, including his innovation of Sunday schools, Bala became a leading centre of Methodism.

Founded by Roger Mortimer around 1310, Bala was the last of the medieval boroughs – deliberately planted urban settlements – to be established in Wales. During the eighteenth century the town became famous as a place where woollen clothing was made, including gloves and some 200,000 pairs of stockings each year. This needed a large supply of wool!

Bala is central to the history of religion in Wales, as an important centre of Methodism. In 1800 fifteen-year-old Mary Jones, a weaver's daughter from Llanfihangel-y-Pennant, walked 25 miles over mountain tracks barefoot to buy a Bible from the Reverend Thomas Charles of Bala. Her determination inspired him to propose the foundation of The British and Foreign Bible Society, to supply copies to the poor. Mary's Bible is now in the society's archives at Cambridge University.

Bala is an ideal base for exploring the region of Penllyn – the 'head of the lake' – and wider Snowdonia. There's a superb choice of accommodation: from farm B&Bs where you experience something of rural life to country-house hotels, restaurants with rooms, self-catering cottages, caravan parks, campsites and bunkhouses.

It's a great place to enjoy the great outdoors. Walkers and cyclists will find routes at whatever level of exertion suits them. The mountains at the southern end of the lake – Aran Benllyn and Aran Fawddwy – are the ultimate challenge, at almost 3,000 feet. There's a sailing club on the lake, with a varied fleet of dinghies and windsurfing is popular too. For canoeing and white-water rafting, the National White Water Centre on the river Tryweryn has the incomparable advantage of a slalom course that can be turned into a raging torrent at the flick of a switch in the control room of the vast dam at Llyn Celyn upriver.

Bala enjoys a scenic location on the shore of Bala Lake (Llyn Tegid) which, at four miles long, is Wales's largest natural lake. But this view shows the real reason for Bala's existence as a market town; the valley of the river Dee, which flows out of Bala Lake, and the surrounding uplands form a region of high agricultural productivity.

The narrow-gauge Bala Lake Railway runs along the southern side of the lake to Llanuwchllyn at the other end. The views across the water to Bala and the peaks of Arenig Fawr are spectacular.

Opposite top: The Norman motte – Tomen y Bala – provides views over the rooftops of the town to the lake and the mountains beyond. It is now a public garden with a gentle spiral path leading to the top.

Opposite below: Bala has a range of shops that appeal both to visitors and to the householders, gardeners and farmers of the area.

Above: George Borrow visited the White Lion Royal Hotel on the High Street during his tour of 'Wild Wales' and was moved to write very favourably of the breakfast he received there. The incorporation of the word 'royal' into the name derives from a visit by Queen Victoria.

Opposite top left: Thomas Edward Ellis MP (1859-99) was elected as a Liberal Member of Parliament in Gladstone's government, in 1886. He was an advocate of public access to the countryside and self-government for Wales. He died at the age of forty, from typhoid contracted during a visit to Egypt, and is commemorated by this dynamic statue on Bala's High Street.

Opposite top right: In common with many towns, Bala has a heritage trail marked by plaques marking interesting buildings and commemorating famous people. Wherever you visit, it's always worth popping into the tourist information centre or library to see if the council or a local historical society has devised such a trail, with an accompanying leaflet to guide you round.

Opposite below left: Characterful street furniture – lamps, railings, door-knockers, postboxes and much else – adds to the appeal of our historic towns.

Opposite below right: The Cywain rural-heritage centre is an exciting new venture that displays countryside craft alongside contemporary art, including powerful sculptures by local artists. It hosts many events including a food festival and falconry displays.

Brecon

Brecon is located at the crossing point of the A470, the main north-south trunk road running the whole length of Wales, and the east-west A40. The main peaks of the Brecon Beacons are some five miles to the south-west and the town has many shops, pubs, hotels and guest houses serving those who come here to enjoy the great outdoors. Brecon has a population of 7,901.

Market days
Tuesday, Friday and Saturday

Livestock was always the fundamental commodity of a market town. McCartneys – an independent family firm established in 1874 – runs frequent auctions of cattle, sheep, horses and farm machinery at its markets in Brecon, Knighton, Kington, Ludlow and Worcester.

The name Brecon derives from Brycheiniog, the land of Brychan, a fifth-century Welsh chieftain. The Welsh name Aberhonddu tells of a confluence of the rivers Honddu and Usk, a good site for a town in terms of communications, defence and agriculture. Bernard de Neufmarché – the Norman Lord of Brecon and half-brother of William the Conqueror – established his motte-and-bailey township in 1093 on a hill overlooking the junction of the two rivers.

The town grew in a southerly direction between the castle and the rivers. It was once defended by solid town walls, having five gates, but these were demolished during the Civil Wars. The Acts of Union made Brecon a county town; its residents and merchants enjoyed a high level of prosperity during the centuries that followed.

Many of the town centre's fine buildings date from the eighteenth and nineteenth centuries, when Brecon thrived as a market town for the farming region that surrounds it. The Brecon Agricultural Society, which met at the Golden Lion Inn to look after the interests of its members, was the first of its kind in Wales. Brecon remains a significant centre of commerce; it has numerous attractive shops, many pubs and cafés, and one of the largest livestock markets in Wales. The Brecon Jazz Festival, with its carnival parade through the town, is a highlight each August.

Brecon also has a long-established military tradition. The South Wales Borderers (who distinguished themselves in many conflicts, including the Zulu Wars) and other Welsh regiments are remembered at the Regimental Museum of The Royal Welsh at the Barracks, located on The Watton. The Mandalay Company of the Gurkha Regiment has been based at Dering Lines, just outside the town, since 1974. Its soldiers are respected members of the community, they were made Honorary Citizens of Brecon in 1985 and hold an impressive commemorative parade each September, with their families resplendent in the national dress of Nepal.

Brecon enjoys an outstandingly
scenic location within sight
of the mountain peaks of the
Brecon Beacons.

The town centre has a high concentration of art and antiques shops. Artbeat Brecon is an organisation formed to promote galleries and cultural enterprises; its members produce paintings, fabrics, sculpture, glassware, jewellery and distinctive gifts – the Tourist Information Centre has a leaflet and map. There is also an excellent old-fashioned toyshop called 'Cariad', on The Watton, stocked with wooden toys and puzzles, traditional dolls and soft toys, and much else that needs no battery!

THE MARKET HALL

The arched frontage of the Market Hall, built in 1857 to a design by T H Wyatt, leads to a hallway with permanent shops to either side, then to a larger hall with a variety of stalls.

When he established the town, Bernard de Neufmarché also founded a Benedictine priory on a pre-existing site of Celtic Christianity, with its church dedicated to St John the Evangelist. This was much enlarged during medieval times and there has been continuity of worship on the site ever since. With the disestablishment of the Church in Wales in 1920 – with its own Archbishop, separate from Canterbury – St John's church became the cathedral of the new diocese of Swansea and Brecon. Its many treasures include the largest Norman font in the UK.

Brecon has many listed buildings. There are some characteristically Tudor buildings at Buckingham Place, once home to the Bishop of St David's, and several handsome seventeenth and eighteenth-century houses on Lion Street. The red-brick Georgian facade and wrought-iron railings of No. 4 Lion Street, formerly known as The Country Club and dating from around 1750, are especially impressive.

Builth Wells

Builth Wells is a classic nodal point, of the sort you might remember from geography lessons at school. Good roads converge here from north, west and south Wales, along the Wye and Irfon valleys – making this a logical location for the Royal Welsh Showground. Builth Wells has a population of 2,352.

Shows

Royal Welsh Smallholder and Garden Festival – mid May; Royal Welsh Show – mid July; Royal Welsh Winter Fair – late November / early December

The Royal Welsh Show is Britain's largest and most popular agricultural event, attracting as many as 60,000 visitors per day over four days in July each year. Cattle, sheep, goats, pigs, horses, ponies and poultry are judged in their own rings and pavilions, before the champion animals form the huge parade of winning stock in the main ring at the end of each afternoon. The accolade of Supreme Champion at The Royal Welsh is the ultimate goal for many a farmer and breeder.

The origins of Builth Wells lie in the cantref, or hundred, of Buallt, which loosely translates as 'ox hill'. This was part of a region known as Rhwng Gŵy a Hafren – Twixt Wye and Severn. It was conquered by the Normans in 1095 and the de Breos family became Lords of Builth. It was nearby, at Cilmeri, that Prince Llywelyn ap Gruffudd met his death at the hands of Edward I's troops.

Only the foundations now remain of the large castle built here by Edward I. He granted the town a charter in 1277 as a Royal Borough. It grew steadily into a small market town, despite the Great Plague which ravaged the area in the 1350s, and a catastrophe in 1690 when the homes of some forty families were destroyed by fire.

The Welsh name Llanfair-ym-Muallt refers to St Mary's church in the region of Buallt. The English form 'Builth' is clearly an approximation of Buallt, without the need to pronounce the 'll' sound that characterises the Welsh language.

Springs of healing mineral waters were discovered here during the eighteenth century and, from the 1830s onwards, these became popular. Large numbers of visitors came to Builth to take the waters, especially after the arrival of the railway in 1860. In a fine example of Victorian marketing spin, the name of the town was augmented to Builth Wells. The Park Wells had salt water and the Glanne Wells had a high sulphur content; each was efficacious in the treatment of specific ailments.

The appeal of healing springs has declined but, more than ever, Builth continues to fulfil its role in the rural economy. It still has a livestock market and is home to The Royal Welsh Show, Wales's biggest agricultural marketplace by far, which is attended by many thousands of people each July.

The hilly terrain around Builth Wells highlights the importance of the valley floor as a transport route through the upland country, and of a solid river bed capable of providing good foundations for a bridge. In past centuries, whoever controlled the roads and crossing points would be well placed to rule a wider region.

The Royal Welsh Show is not all about farming; there are more than 1,000 trade stands and pavilions with displays covering food and drink, forestry, horticulture, garden design, arts and crafts, pets, outdoor pursuits, bee-keeping and much else. Other events held here include the Smallholder and Garden Festival in mid May, horse and pony competitions, dog shows and antiques fairs. The Royal Welsh Winter Fair at the beginning of December is the most important winter event in the farming calendar.

Left: The town's livestock market also continues to thrive, holding busy sales year-round.

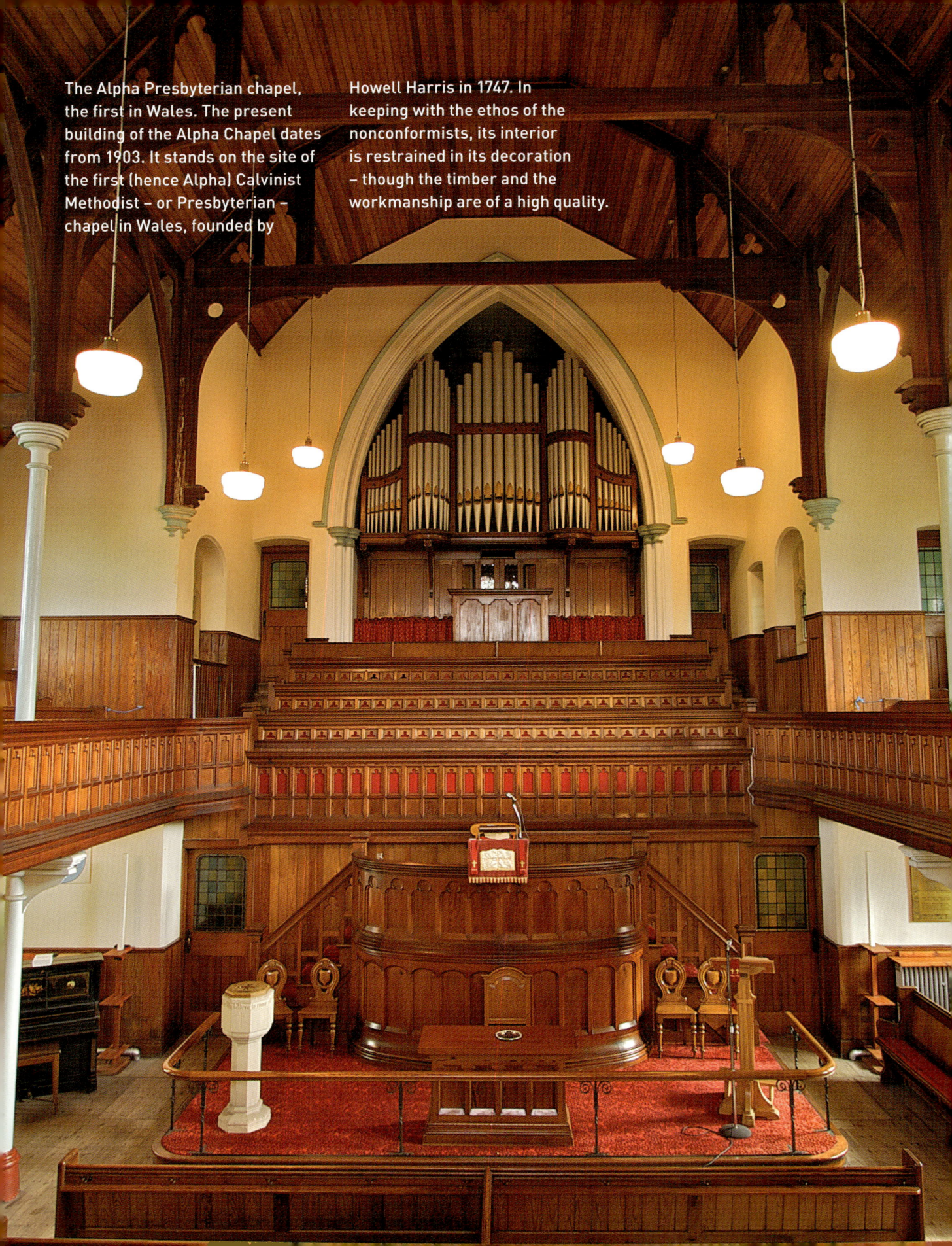

The Alpha Presbyterian chapel, the first in Wales. The present building of the Alpha Chapel dates from 1903. It stands on the site of the first (hence Alpha) Calvinist Methodist – or Presbyterian – chapel in Wales, founded by Howell Harris in 1747. In keeping with the ethos of the nonconformists, its interior is restrained in its decoration – though the timber and the workmanship are of a high quality.

Above: The town centre; Land Rovers, horse boxes and farm vehicles are ubiquitous in and around our market towns. They remind us that the people who live and work in rural Wales perform a valuable role in feeding the nation and in providing us with food security in the face of climate change and other potential threats. The narrow streets of Builth are famous far and wide for their excellent Christmas lights; they also echo to the annual Festival of Dance each May and a Carnival each June.

Right: Builth's dignified War memorial, dedicated to all of the Services, stands in carefully tended gardens. An iron Pill Box shelter, used locally during the Second World War, reminds us of the readiness of the Home Guard to defend the nation.

TO THE
HONOURED MEMORY
OF HER SONS,
WHO DIED DURING
THE WAR IN
SOUTH AFRICA,
1899 — 1902,
CARMARTHENSHIRE
DEDICATES
THIS MEMORIAL

Carmarthen

Carmarthen is fifteen miles beyond the western end of the M4 motorway and about the same distance west of Llandeilo, along the A40. Lampeter is twenty-three miles north-westward along the A485. Carmarthen has a rail station on the line linking Cardiff, Swansea and Pembrokeshire and a population of 13,130.

Market days

Wednesday and Saturday, and the new indoor market is open Monday to Saturday

The Guildhall was designed in 1767 by Sir Robert Taylor and stands on the site of a Tudor hall. The lower level, once open to the street, accommodated market stalls. The memorial commemorates soldiers lost during the Boer War.

Carmarthen is in the lower, tidal part of the river Tywi, at the lowest bridging point achievable by medieval civil engineers. The open sea is almost ten miles away (including bends in the river) so that, although Carmarthen served as a port for small vessels until the 1920s, its character is that of an inland market town.

The Romans built a fort here around AD75 and their regional capital – Moridunum, the Sea Fort – grew around it. By AD220 the town was encircled by stone walls, the remains of which are discernible in the street layout, and an amphitheatre also survives. Carmarthen claims to be the oldest town in Wales; the other Roman capital – Venta Silurum (Caerwent), near Chepstow – has some of the best-preserved Roman city walls in Europe, but is now a small village.

The town's Welsh name, Caerfyrddin, may have evolved from the Latin Moridunum into the Welsh forms of môr (sea) and din (fort). It is also linked to the legend that the similar-sounding Myrddin (Merlin the Magician) was born here; did he perhaps take his name from the place?

As so often, it was the Normans who set the town on course for expansion. Early in the twelfth century, they built a castle overlooking the river and a new town began to grow around it. By 1290, under Edward I, it was the main centre of administration in south-west Wales. The old and new parts of Carmarthen were amalgamated, as a borough, in 1546.

By the late-sixteenth century, Carmarthen had more than 2,000 residents and was the largest town in Wales, reputedly the first to attain a higher population than Venta Silurum. It held that position for two centuries, until the Industrial Revolution attracted the masses to the south-Wales coalfield and the seaports that served it.

Carmarthen's street layout radiates from the top of a hill, near the castle gatehouse. A statue in front of the Angel Vaults commemorates Sir William Nott, a British commander in India, whose father was innkeeper of the Ivybush Inn. Nott Square, created in his honour in 1846, was previously the market square. The old market hall was replaced in 2009 by a shiny new one. Many of the familiar stalls remain; their owners know many of their customers by their first names and always make time for a chat.

HAMILTONS RESTAURANT

ROBERT LICKLEY *Licensed to sell Beer, Wines, Spirits & Tobacco*

Hamiltons • Wine • Bar & Restaurant

Main Menu

Starters
Salad Bowl £1.95
Homemade Soup of the Day £2.95
Homemade Chicken Liver Pate £4.50
Atlantic Prawn Cocktail £4.95
Panfried Mushroom in Garlic £4.95

House Specialities
Sweet Chicken Curry £9.95
Homemade Beef Lasagne Verdi £9.25
Chicken Stroganoff £9.95
Stir-fried Chicken + Vegetables in Sweet + Sour £9.95
1/4 Duck in Plum, Honey + Ginger Sauce £9.95
1/2 Duck in Plum, Honey + Ginger Sauce £13.95
Chicken Breast in Italian Sauce £10.95
Chicken Breast in Mushroom + Tarragon Sauce £10.95
Chicken Breast in Garlic + Mushroom Sauce £10.95

Chargrills
Pork Loin Steaks in Garlic Mushroom Sauce £9.95
10oz Gammon Steak with egg + pineapple £9.95
Celtic 10oz Sirloin Steak £15.95
Celtic 8oz Fillet Steak £13.95

Seafood
Whole Tail Breaded Scampi £9.25
Fillet of Cod in Batter or Breadcrumbs £9.95
Fantastic Fish Pie £9.95

Vegetarian
Homemade Vegetable Lasagne £9.95
Mushroom Stroganoff £9.95
Norwegian Mushroom Bake £8.50
Stir-fried Vegetable Curry £9.25

Salads
Cheddar Cheese + Pineapple £5.95
Homecooked Ham £5.95
Home Roasted Turkey £5.95
Atlantic Prawn £6.95

Side Orders
White French Bread £1.00
Garlic Bread £1.20
Plain or Garlic Mushrooms £2.95
Onion Rings £2.45
Stir-fried Mixed Vegetables £2.95
Salad from Salad Bar £2.95
Pepper Sauce, Italian Sauce or Garlic Mushroom Sauce £1.95

Every effort is made to ensure that all items on the menu are available. However, certain items may be unavailable due to demand. We reserve the right to amend the menu and prices at any time. All weights, where stated, are approximate before cooking.

Children's Menu

Sweet Chicken Curry £4.50
Beef Lasagne £4.50
Vegetable Lasagne £4.50
Roast Turkey with Veg £4.50
Chicken Nuggets £3.95
2 Sausages £3.95
2 Fish Fingers £3.95

All meals come with chips, rice or new potatoes and a free glass of squash.
- Under 14's Only -

Early Evening Special

Served between 6pm and 7pm
2 Course £11.95
3 Course £13.95

Starters
Homemade Soup
Homemade Chicken Liver Pate.
Panfried Garlic Mushrooms
Salad Bowl Selection

Main Course
Fillet of Sewin in Lemon + Dill Sauce
Vegetable Lasagne
2 Pork Cutlets in BBQ Sauce
Sweet Chicken Curry
10oz Gammon Steak with Pineapple
Steak + Mushroom Casserole with Veg
Served with Chips, Jacket, Rice or New Potatoes unless otherwise stated.

Desserts
Choice of dessert on display.

Today's Specials

Starters
Warm Goats Cheese Salad on a Crouton £4.50
Sewin Fishcakes with a sweet chilli dip on a bed of leaves £4.95
Cod Goujon's with a Sweet Chilli Dip on a bed of Mixed Leaves £4.95

Main Course
1/2 Roast Chicken with BBQ Sauce or Garlic Butter £6.95
Fillet Steak in Pepper Sauce £12.95
Sewin Fishcakes with Sweet Chilli dip £7.95
6oz Celtic Sirloin Steak £7.95
Penclawdd Cockles + Laverbread Bake £8.95

New Season Fillet of Towy Sewin with Lemon + Parsley Sauce £13.95

The town has some great pubs and restaurants. During the nineteenth century, Carmarthen had an amazing 150 taverns which were 'open all hours' on market days! The sign on the Drovers Arms hotel reflects the town's position on the ancient livestock routes. Carmarthen's taverns were once noisy and riotous haunts of drovers and farmhands; these "hippies" celebrating a birthday at the Angel Vaults (now a restaurant) could hardly be more different!

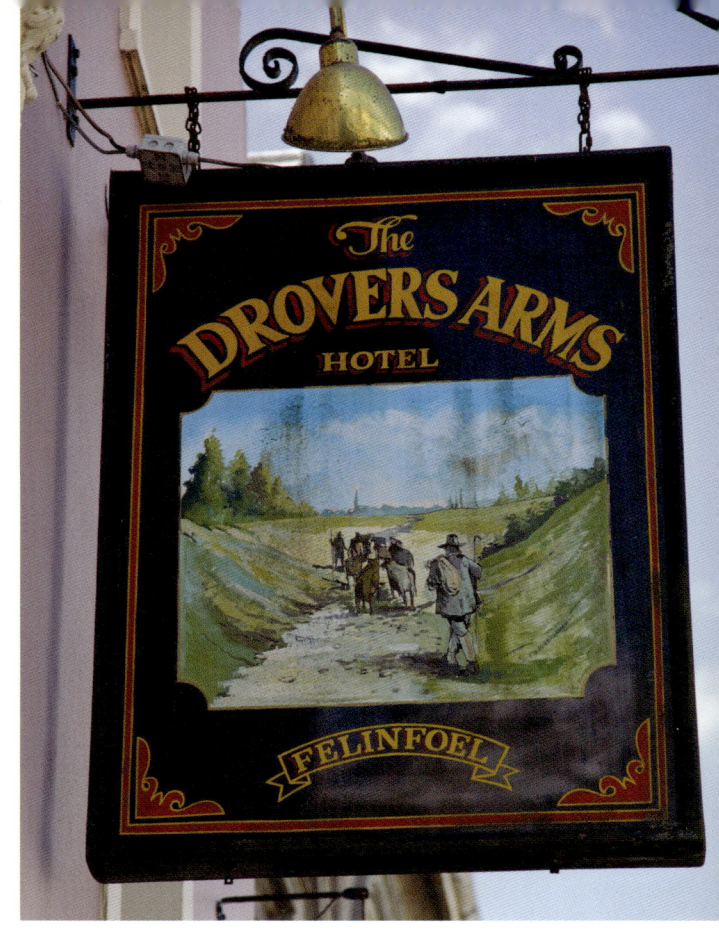

Long seen as the capital of south-west Wales, Carmarthen has buildings that reflect its rapid growth during the nineteenth century; its population grew from around 5,000 in 1800 to over 10,000 fifty years later. As well as being a market town, it also became an important centre for printing, publishing and education. Wales's second weekly newspaper, the Carmarthen Journal, was established here in 1810. The Queen Elizabeth Grammar School, the Presbyterian College, Trinity College (now part of the University of Wales) and the Carmarthen School of Art placed the town on the educational map.

More recently, Carmarthen has grown to a substantial size, thanks to its importance as a county town. The largest building is the headquarters of Carmarthenshire County Council, designed by Sir Percy Thomas in the style of a French château in 1935, and eventually completed in 1955. Shields on its frontages represent the various council functions. The foundations of much of the castle lie beneath.

Chepstow

Wales's south-eastern gateway since Saxon times, Chepstow stands near the western end of the older of the two bridges across the Severn estuary, where ferries previously operated. It is also the gateway to the lower part of the Wye Valley, a designated Area of Outstanding Natural Beauty. Tintern Abbey is minutes away; Caerwent, the Roman Venta Silurum, is just to the west; and the Forest of Dean is to the north-east. Chepstow has a population of 10,821.

Market days
Produce market in Beaufort Square Thursday and Friday; Sunday market at Chepstow Racecourse (spring through to autumn, and at Christmas)

Chepstow Racecourse, just north of the town, is the home of Wales's most prestigious horse race – the Welsh National – along with numerous other meetings held throughout the year. The midsummer Ladies' Evening is especially popular. Crowds also flock to the open-air Sunday Markets, where you will find all manner of clothing, crafts, tools, household items and food.

Following the conquest of 1066, the Normans moved quickly to establish their hold over southern England and the lowland regions of Wales. As early as 1067 they had already built a small wooden fort at Chepstow, from which they consolidated their domination by building the substantial stone castle and the town walls.

Chepstow was William Fitz Osbern's centre of command, from which he controlled the kingdom of Gwent. The castle, a symbolic and powerful deterrent as well as a physical base, occupies a spectacular position on a vertical cliff cut into limestone by the river Wye. Fresh water was raised in buckets from a convenient spring on the river bank, a vital resource in times both of peace and of potential siege. The Great Tower was completed around 1075 and is the castle's dominating feature. It echoes the design of that at Falaise in Normandy and is the earliest reliably datable secular stone building in Britain.

The Wye estuary is tidal here and the town served as a seaport for many centuries, giving access to the Severn estuary, the Bristol Channel and the open sea in one direction and upriver to Tintern and beyond in the other. It was also a centre for fishing – the Wye remains one of the UK's prime rivers for salmon.

The relative narrowness of the river and its helpfully rocky banks also made this a good place to build bridges. The elegant, iron-arched road bridge was constructed in 1816; the original railway bridge of 1852 was designed by Brunel; the modern road bridges across the Severn and the Wye, which carry the M48 motorway, date from 1966.

Today, Chepstow has an air of comfortable prosperity underlined by a tangible feeling of history. It is a thriving town in itself but is also sought after as a pleasant place from which to commute to Cardiff, Newport and Bristol.

Here is the reason that Chepstow stands where it does. The river Wye in its lower reaches, just before joining the sea, has obligingly cut a narrow gorge through the limestone. The advantages are clear; the geography provides a bridging point with good foundations either side and a tremendous defensive position on an imposing clifftop, ideal for the building of a castle.

ARTOIS

HERBERT

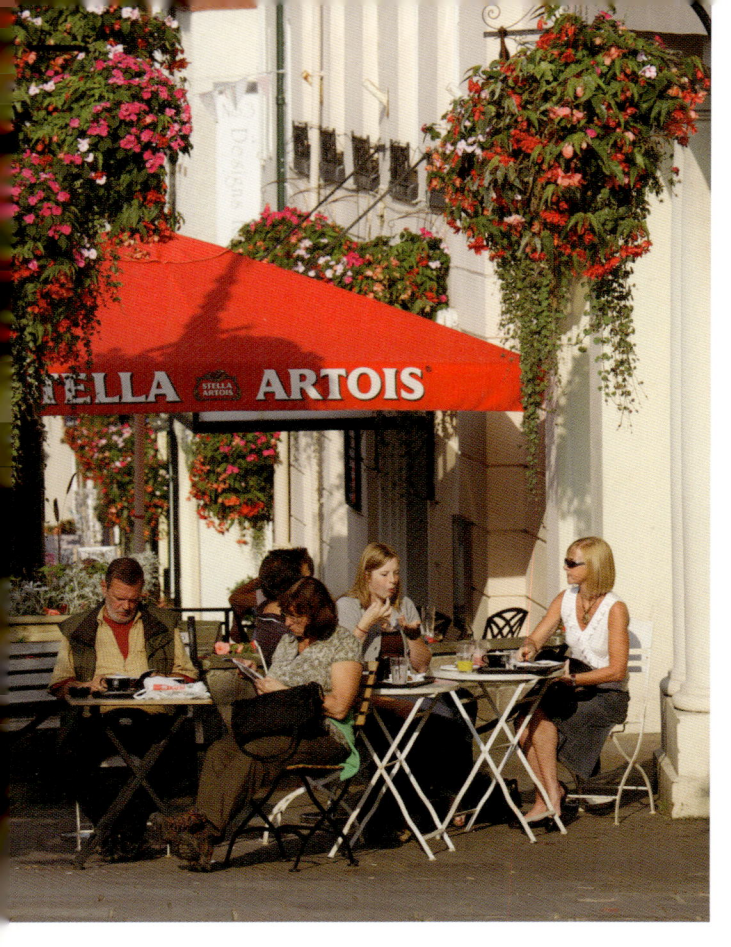

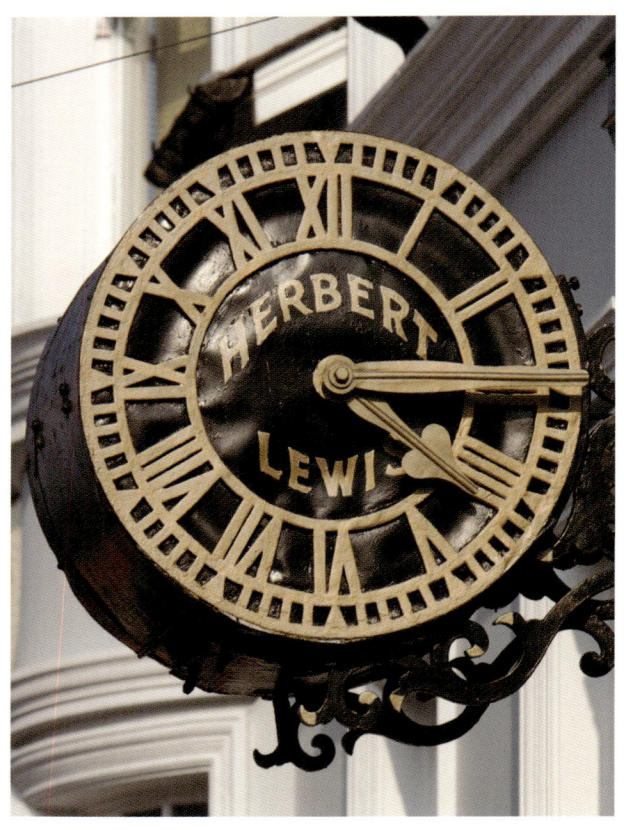

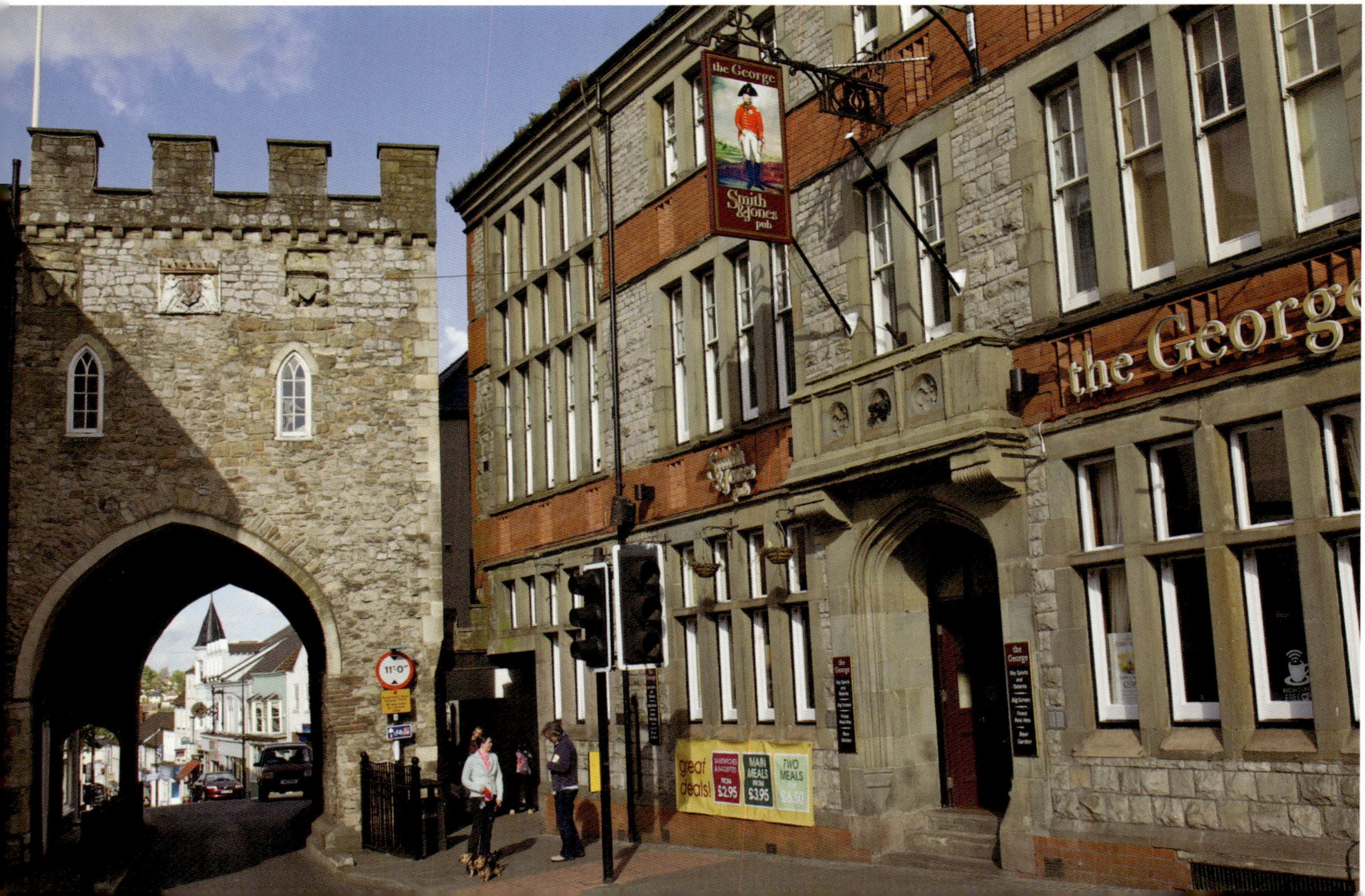
the George
the George
Smith &Jones pub

Opposite below: The Town Gate provided a fortified entry point at the western end of the town, furthest from the castle. As with every market town, Chepstow has some fine old pubs and former coaching inns, where stagecoach passengers, drivers and the hard-working horses could rely upon finding comfortable quarters and welcome sustenance during their arduous journeys.

The town centre reflects medieval priorities; it was safe to live and conduct business here within the town walls. High Street has an attractive variety of buildings, street furniture and public artworks.

St Mary Street is home to a cluster of appealing art, antiques and fashion shops, and several restaurants.

The occupants of Chepstow Castle must have derived considerable peace-of-mind from knowing that they were protected by a vertical cliff on one side and solid walls on the other. From 1067, until the seventeenth century, the fortress grew along its narrow cliff-top ledge. As military architecture evolved, the medieval battlements that provided arrow slots for archers were superseded by parapets giving clear lines-of-fire for musketeers. The walls were thickened to resist cannon balls and were adapted further during the Civil War. Chepstow has the oldest castle doors in Europe, made of solid oak and over 800 years old. They were removed in 1962 for safe keeping in the castle's museum.

The turbulent history of Chepstow Castle is brought to life during exciting and educational re-enactments by local societies. The peaceful aspects of life in a medieval encampment are illustrated, as well as the clash and chaos of battle.

Cowbridge

Cowbridge lies in the Vale of Glamorgan, some six miles south-west of J34 on the M4 motorway, just off the A48 midway between Cardiff and Bridgend. It is surrounded by attractive villages and numerous castles and historic sites. The Glamorgan Heritage Coast is just to the south. Cowbridge has a population of 4,182.

Market days
First and third Saturday of each month

Cowbridge, the market town for the Vale of Glamorgan, occupies a sheltered location of exactly the kind conjured up by the word "vale". It really does nestle snugly on the valley floor, overlooked by gentle hills. It has expanded beyond its historic core and nowadays offers attractive housing and a high quality of life for its fortunate residents.

The attractions of the Vale of Glamorgan, particularly its suitability for agriculture, have been evident since Roman times. Archaeologists have made significant finds here, including the remains of houses and shops, pottery and metal artefacts. This is indicative of a settlement on the site of Cowbridge where the Roman road, the Via Julia, crossed the river Thaw. As well as giving us good roads and underfloor heating, the Romans also planted vineyards, a tradition that continues in the region today.

The Norman Lord of Glamorgan Richard de Clare founded the Borough of Cowbridge, which received its Charter as Longa Villa or long town in 1254. It was a logical choice of location for a new centre of commerce, with all its supporting trades and crafts. Cowbridge is unusual among Norman settlements in having no castle of its own; de Clare's seat was at nearby Llanblethian. The town soon acquired substantial stone walls, of which segments including the South Gate, where tolls were levied on market days, remain.

The medieval town thrived, as one would expect from its advantageous position amid fruitful farmland. It acquired an air of prosperity and independence and, although the population diminished during the eighteenth century, it gained status and respectability as the "capital of the vale".

Nearby Cardiff's spectacular expansion into the world's largest coal port, during the late-nineteenth and early-twentieth centuries, altered the destiny of the Vale of Glamorgan. Merchants, shipowners and other professions involved in the boom came looking for pleasant places to live, away from the noise and grime of the seaport. Cowbridge grew in linear fashion along the road known as the Portway (now the A48). In more recent decades it has gradually expanded into the surrounding countryside. The historical ambience of the town, and the scenic delights of the vale, continue to make Cowbridge a popular place in which to live.

The most distinctive attribute of Cowbridge is its marvellous range of shops, galleries, restaurants and cafés, where high standards of quality and service prevail. Shoppers enjoy a refreshing change from the bland standardisation of today's typical High Street. Christmas is an especially popular time to visit, to buy gifts, food and wine, and to enjoy the seasonal atmosphere. The Old Wool Barn Arts and Crafts Centre is home to several talented artists, along with shops specialising in cake decoration and fine chocolate.

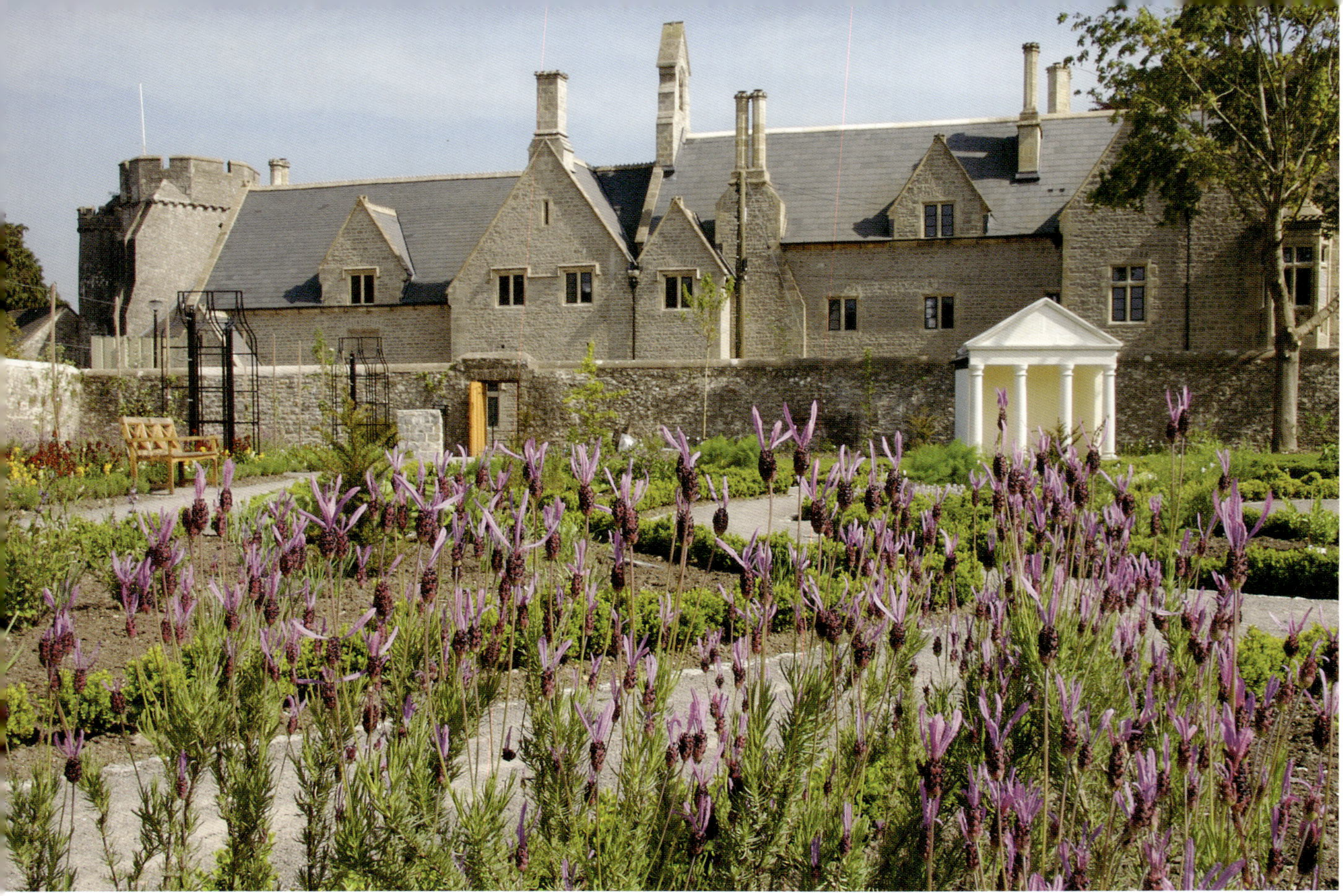

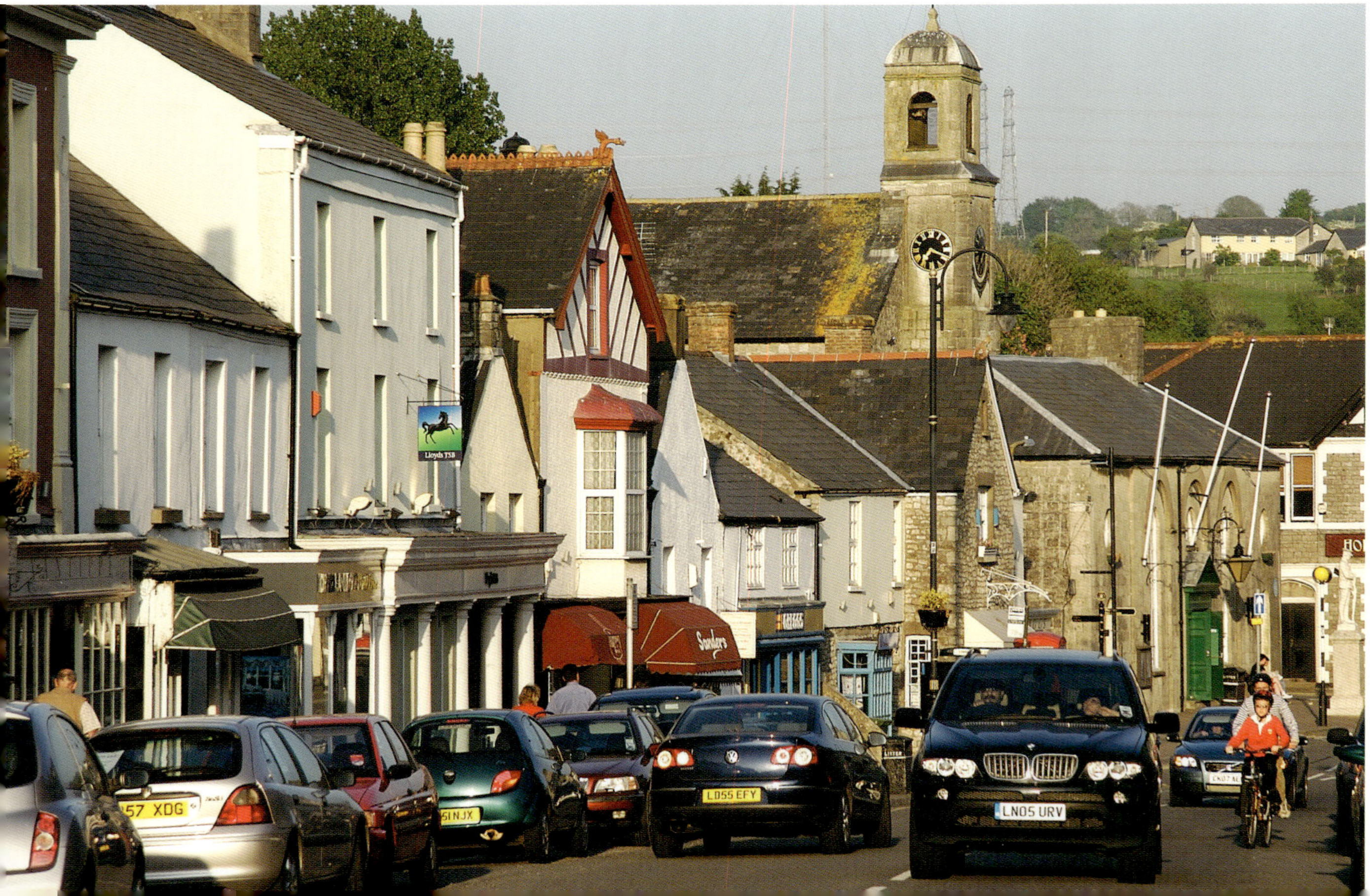
Lloyds TSB
57 XDG
LD55 EFY
LN05 URV

Opposite above: The Cowbridge Physic Garden is a relatively recent addition to the attractions of the town. In this walled oasis of calm you will find a fascinating range of medicinal plants, grouped according to the ailments and regions of the body for which they are efficacious. It stands in the former walled garden of Cowbridge Grammar School, seen in the background. This was founded in 1608 and counts actor, director and musician Sir Anthony Hopkins among its former pupils.

The Town Hall has a fine clock, presented in 1836 by the Bishop of Llandaff, a handsome weather vane and a moving war memorial. The town's museum is housed in cells that remain from the prison that previously stood on the site.

Opposite: At the Cowbridge Food Festival and similar events throughout Wales, customers are able to sample the best of local food and meet the people who make it. Prize-winning artisan producers apply great care and skill to the highest-quality ingredients; the resulting taste sets their efforts apart from the ubiquitous high-volume brands found on supermarket shelves.

Left: This is the Wild Fig farm shop in Peterston Super Ely, near Cowbridge. As one of the highly regarded producers of the area, it is famous for its fresh fruit and vegetables grown on the site. It also sells its own ice cream and is soon to begin producing wines from its recently planted vines.

Crickhowell

With the Black Mountains to the north and the Brecon Beacons to the west, Crickhowell occupies a distinctly upland setting. The A40 becomes very narrow here, as it makes a sharp dog-leg turn in front of the Bear Hotel. Here, and throughout mid Wales, be on the lookout for large trucks carrying livestock, hay bales or logs from forestry plantations – and for fast-moving motorcyclists, often on club outings and riding their showpiece machines in a pack. Crickhowell has a population of 2,065.

Market day
Thursday

Crickhowell is the Anglicized form of Crug Hywel, the name of the fortification on the flat-topped hill (known as Table Mountain) above the town. This is the site of an Iron Age hill fort but it has also become associated with Hywel Dda – Hywel the Good – ruler of much of Wales during the mid-tenth century, whose legacy was an effective and enlightened body of law.

The town's central "square" is actually triangular, apparently in a nod to the similar layout found in the home town of the Norman lord Bernard de Neufmarché. Crickhowell was made a Borough in 1281, the market was held on land belonging to the manor, to the benefit of the ruling Pauncefoot family. A general market in the streets of the town is recorded from the early-seventeenth century onwards.

Little remains of Crickhowell's castle, built by the splendidly named Sir Grimbald Pauncefoot in 1272. The structure that survived the vigorous attention of Owain Glyndŵr in 1403 comprises the gatehouse tower, part of the curtain wall and the portcullis gate which were especially strongly built at the time. The name of Standard Street, just off the square, commemorates the occasion in 1485 when Sir Richard Evans raised his standard there and mustered 3,000 men to march to Bosworth Field where they shared in Henry Tudor's victory.

Today Crickhowell presents itself as a Fair Trade town, in which a fair price is paid to producers of food, craft goods and artworks. The promoters of this well-known scheme, which "Guarantees a better deal for Third World producers", are keen to point out that they apply the same philosophy to local suppliers. Alongside tea, coffee, chocolate and other items sourced from overseas, you will find local honey, cakes, apple juice, smoked foods, ice-cream, wine, beer, whisky and much else.

Crickhowell's population is less than that of many a large village, but it nevertheless qualifies as a market town. Its position was determined by the availability of a good spot at which to build a bridge over the river Usk.

The Bear Hotel is one of Wales's most charming coaching inns. Its Georgian frontage, cobbled courtyard and the archway through which horses were led to the stables are evocative of a time when journeys were long and arduous. Today its standards are higher than ever, as reflected in the awards it has received.

The Bridge End Inn (opposite below) incorporates one of the town's three original tollhouses. It is a traditional hostelry providing good food, excellent ales and, as seen here, a welcoming landlord and convivial company.

THE
BEAR

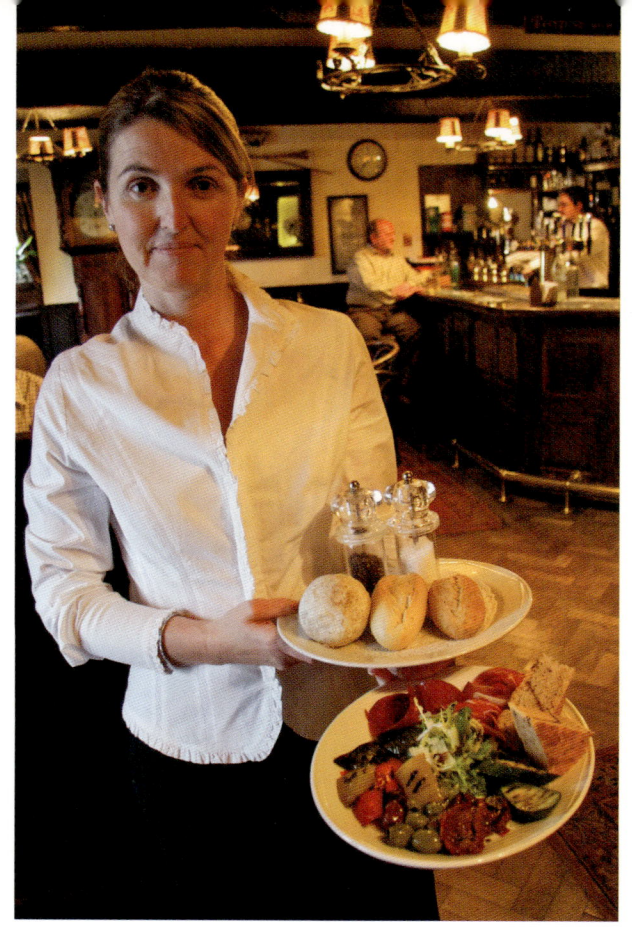

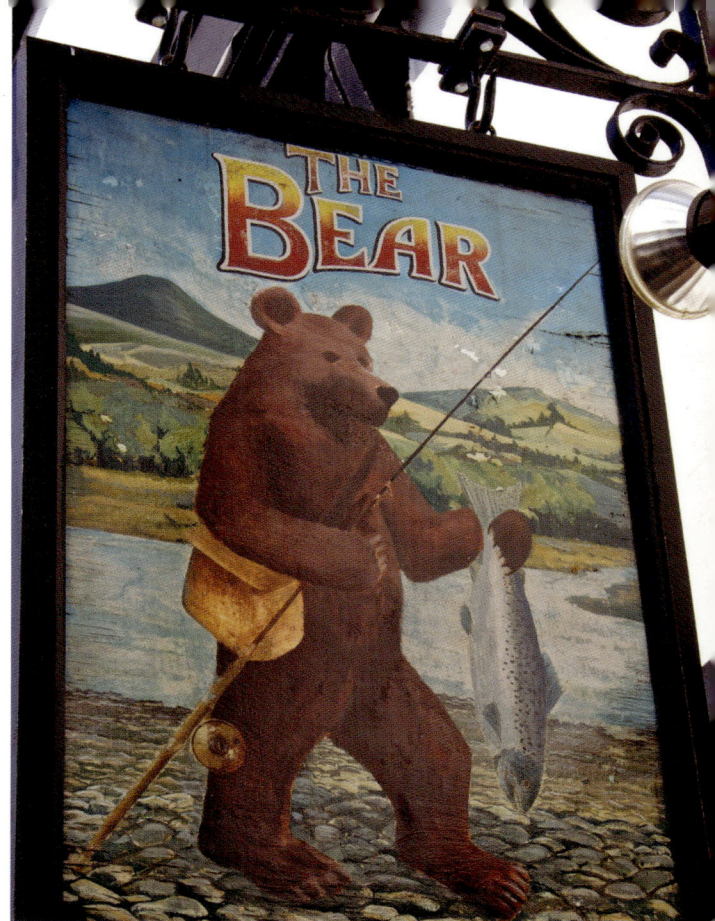

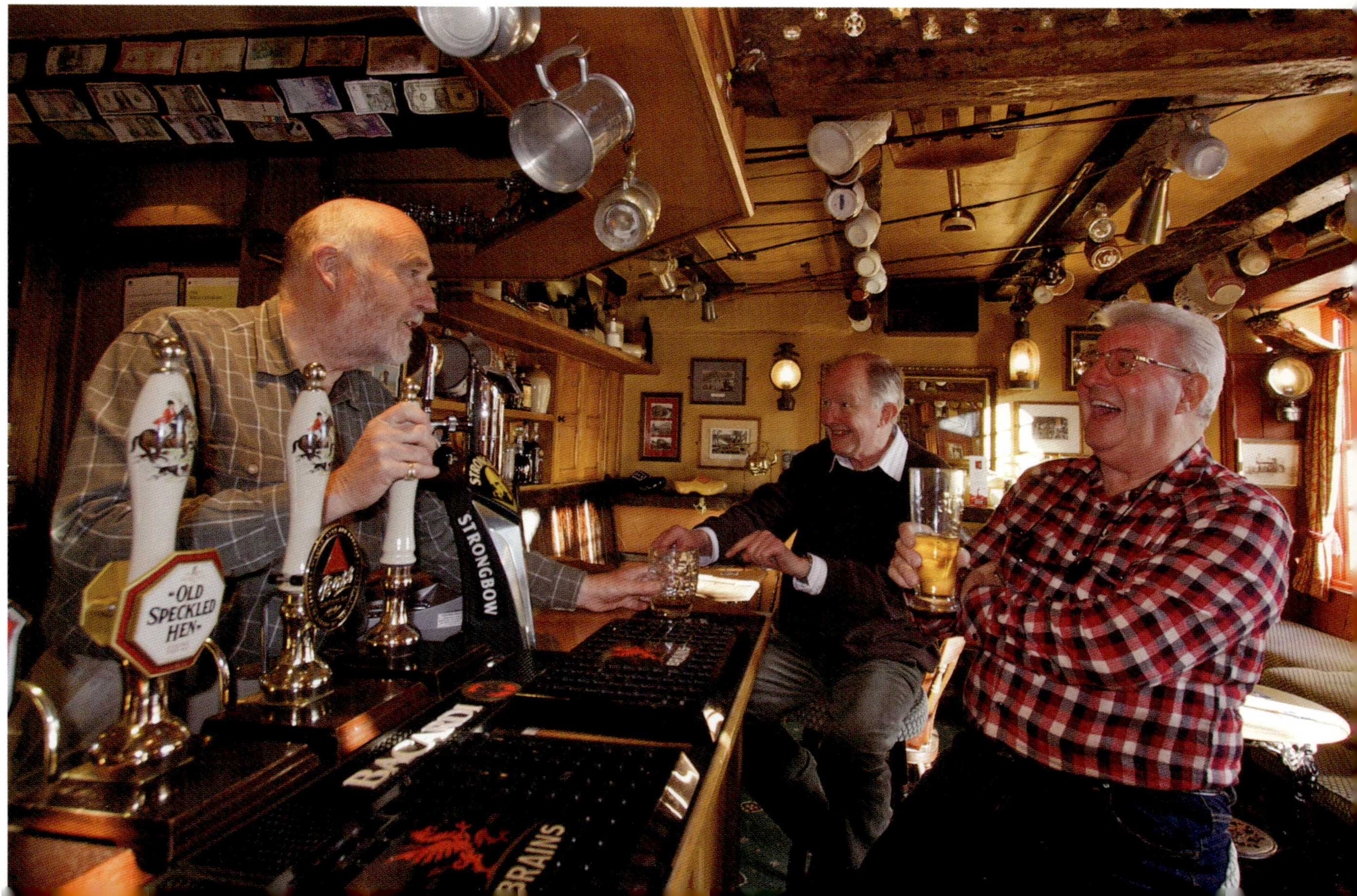
OLD SPECKLED HEN
STRONGBOW
BACARDI
BRAINS

There is a wealth of architectural detail to enjoy in Crickhowell, much of it Georgian in origin. The central window of the pink-washed Dragon Hotel is a local interpretation of the Palladian style.

Left: The White Hart Inn has provided sustenance to travellers on the Brecon road since the sixteenth century. A board listing the tariffs levied on animals and vehicles entering the market town, at the tollhouse that once stood nearby, is displayed on its front wall.

The bridge over the river Usk dates from 1760 and intriguingly (following alterations in 1830, to accommodate the new road south of the river) has thirteen arches on one side and twelve on the other.

In an award-winning example of sensitive development that preserves regional character, these attractive houses at Upper House Farm were built in vernacular style, using suitably rustic-looking local materials during the late-1990s. This was the dawn of the internet age; the site was promoted as a "tele-village" and the houses were ready-wired for home workers which was a pioneering concept at the time. The nearby group of farm buildings, once home to the Rumsey family, has been preserved; the granary contains shops and one of the barns is home to Tools for Self Reliance – an organisation that recycles old tools, for sale and for donation to farmers and craftsmen in the third world.

Dolgellau

Dolgellau is just off the A470 north-to-south Wales trunk road. It is sixteen miles north of Machynlleth, in a more rugged, upland setting. The Mawddach estuary is just to the west. Dolgellau has a population of 2,678.

Market days
Country Market Thursday; Farmers' Market middle Sunday of each month

The construction of St Mary's parish church, dating from 1716, is unusual; dressed-slate blocks overlap at the corners in the style of a log cabin. The Catholic Church, Our Lady of Seven Sorrows, was completed in 1966 thanks to the efforts of the priest, Father Francis Scalpell, who was originally from Malta.

Long an important meeting point of drover's roads, Dolgellau grew as a serf town or a taeogdref during the early Middle Ages. The lack of any master plan is evident in the haphazard layout of the narrow streets and irregularly shaped squares. It is this, along with the grey local stone, that makes the place feel different and gives it such character.

Dolgellau was a centre for the woollen industry during the eighteenth century, when spinning and weaving were hand processes. The river Aran, which descends from the slopes of Cadair Idris, provided power for the fulling mills. Here wool was washed and beaten with wooden mallets to consolidate the fibres, and water was later used for carding and spinning machinery. As the Industrial Revolution gathered pace, Dolgellau's weavers who were working in lofts on the top storeys of the houses became unable to compete with the gigantic mechanised mills of Lancashire and Yorkshire.

Industrialisation, however, also brought with it improvements to roads and railways and for some greater affluence and more leisure time. It became fashionable to follow the example of the Romantic artists and poets (Turner and Wordsworth both visited Wales) by visiting remote, scenic regions. The mountains of Wales were accessible to those who wished to savour the exhilaration of an encounter with what they saw as 'the sublime'. Wild country was seen, for the first time, as being good for the soul, as opposed to being dangerous and terrifying.

Dolgellau responded by reinventing itself as a tourist destination. Guides led mule trips up Cadair Idris and harpists played traditional Welsh airs in the inns of the town. The railway and the motor car brought more people; hotels and guest houses opened to welcome them. Tourism remains an important part of the economy today and visitors ranging from gentle explorers to energetic thrill seekers will find all types of accommodation, from campsites to boutique hotels.

Dolgellau – in the valley of the river Wnion, shaded by Cadair Idris – is a very atmospheric town. The dark stone and slate of its buildings give it a character all of its own, especially in contrast to the vivid colours of autumn.

Eldon Square is the central hub of Dolgellau. The former market hall, Neuadd Idris, is typical of the town's architecture; solid and unornamented but handsome in its contrasting stonework and strong proportions. Tŷ Meirion – formerly London House, a shop selling goods from a London merchant – houses an exhibition about the local Quakers who emigrated to Pennsylvania to escape persecution. The highly regarded women's college at Merion Avenue, Bryn Mawr, Pennsylvania is named after the Quaker farm Bryn Mawr above Dolgellau in Meirionnydd.

Many premises have been adapted to new uses. The old police station is now the stylish Meirionnydd Hotel. The T H Roberts ironmonger's shop is now a popular café, with newspapers to read and board games to play. Many of its original fittings are still in place, it would have been an important source of tools and materials for townsfolk, farmers, quarrymen and the miners who dug for gold at Gwynfynydd, north of Dolgellau. Towns like this once produced their own gas from coal; Dolgellau's gasworks is now a cycle shop and hire centre. The old Town Hall, dated 1606, now accommodates the Sospan restaurant.

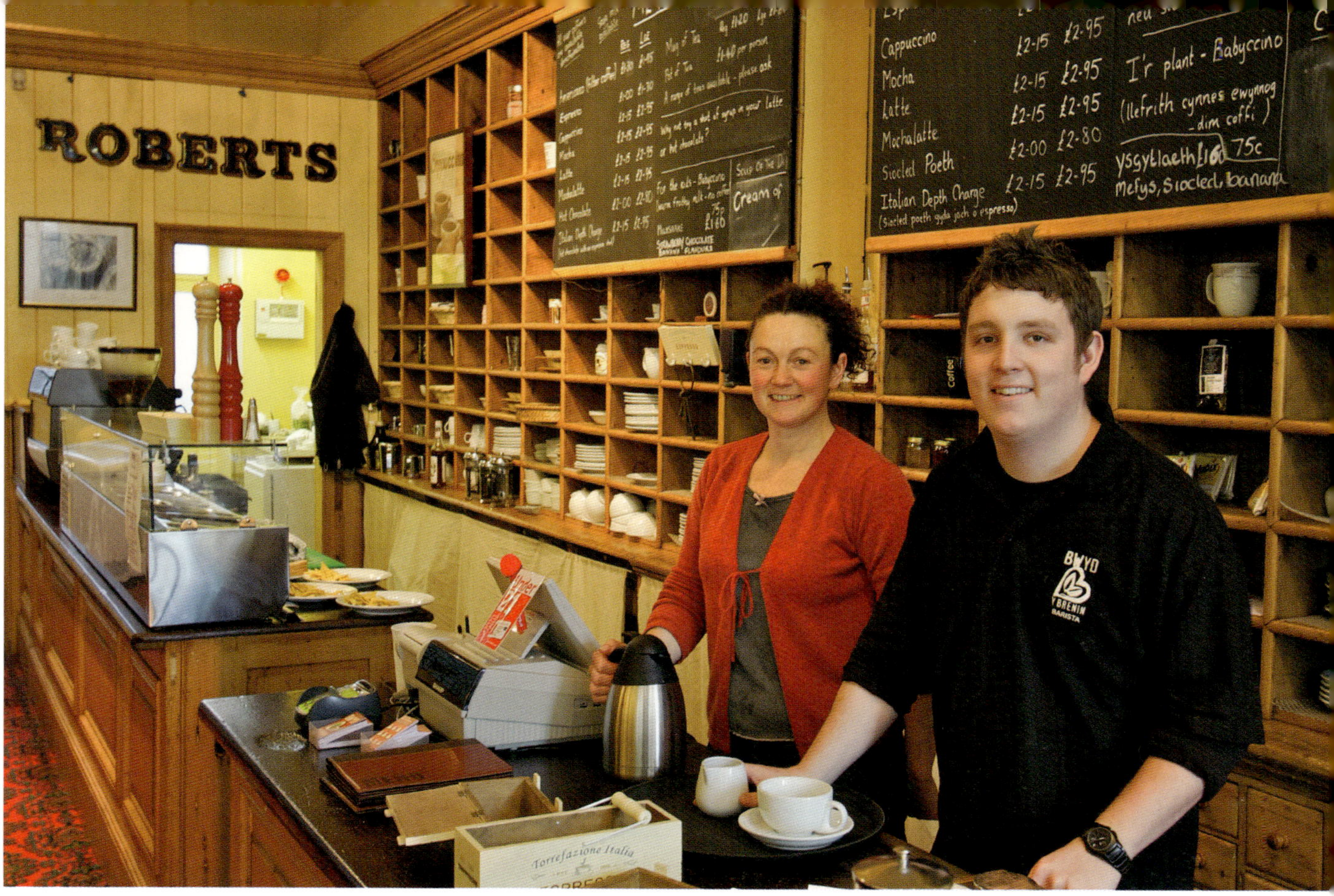
ROBERTS
Cappuccino £2·15 £2·95
Mocha £2·15 £2·95
Latte £2·15 £2·95
Mochalatte £2·15 £2·80
Siocled Poeth £2·00 £2·80
Italian Depth Charge £2·15 £2·95
I'r plant - Babyccino
Torrefazione Italia

Y SOSPAN
BISTRO
WINE BAR
Licensed Restaurant

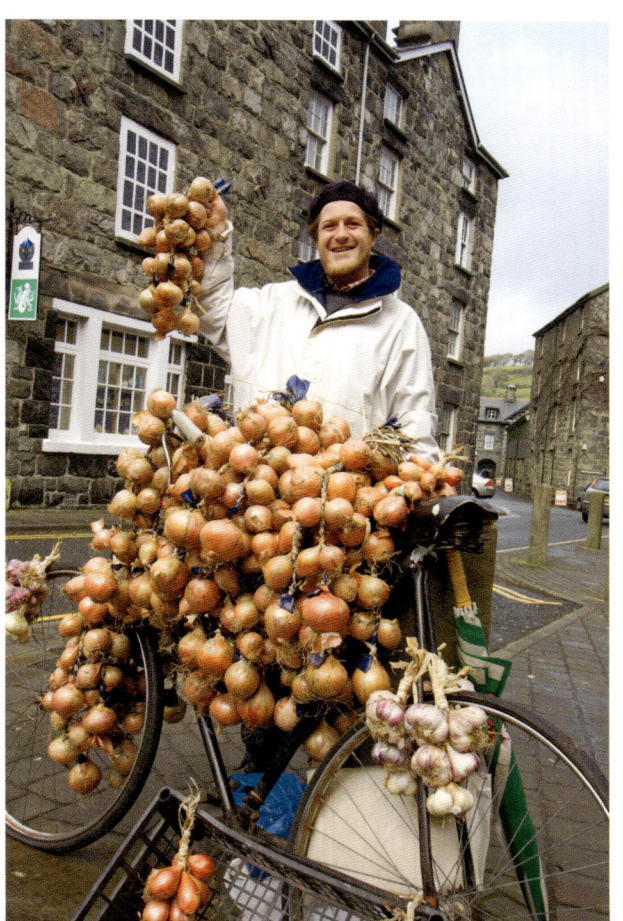

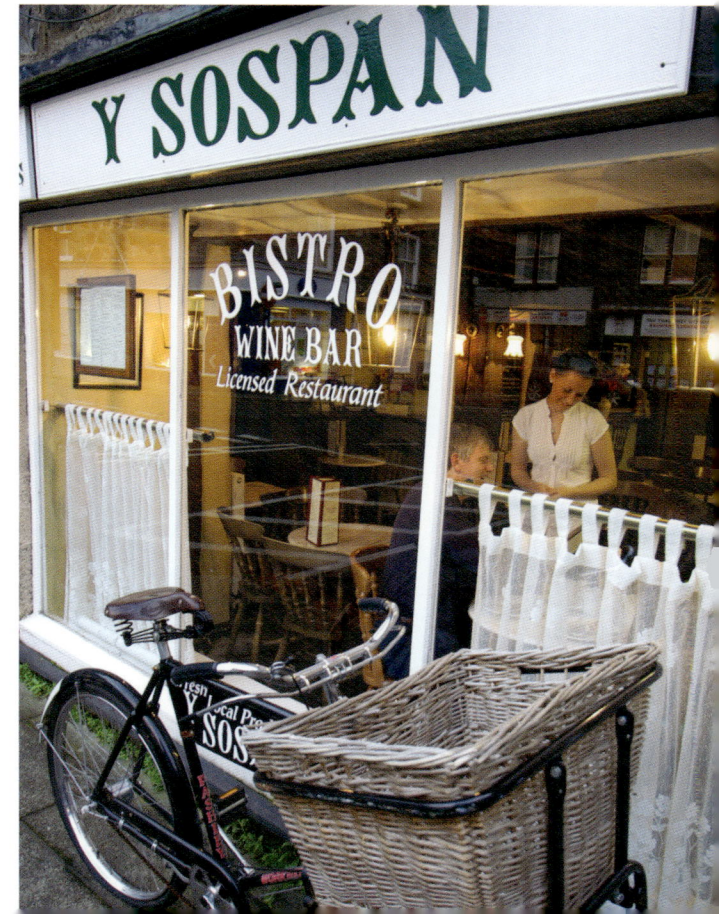

The livestock market attracts farmers and buyers from all over Snowdonia. The market is a social occasion, as well as a place of business; many people enjoy going along even if they are not buying or selling.

Haverfordwest

Haverfordwest is thirty miles west of Carmarthen along the A40, an excellent road that leads to the ferry port at Fishguard, and seven miles north-east of Milford Haven. Haverfordwest has a population of 10,808.

Market days
Riverside Market Monday to Saturday; Farmers' Market every other Friday

A steep hill leads to the upper part of the town, around High Street and Market Street; this is where you will find the Top Town Traders, a group of independent shops including a butcher, an art gallery, a delicatessen and several restaurants.

At the invitation of Henry I Flemish immigrants, who had lost their lands in the Low Countries to flooding, arrived in south-west Wales early in the twelfth century. Their leader, Tancred, built a wooden stronghold here in 1110; the town celebrated its 900th anniversary in 2010. Flemish traders and merchants were also prominent in Tenby, they established an enclave connected by sea to their homeland in what is now Belgium. Tancred is commemorated in the names of streets and houses.

Look at a map of Pembrokeshire and you will see that Haverfordwest, though deep in the rural heart of the county, is accessible along the river Cleddau from Milford Haven. There are records of cargoes as varied as salt, iron, wine, and apples from the Forest of Dean arriving here. Outgoing cargo included coal, slate, butter, oats, wheat, barley, hides and wool. The Old Quay, the Bristol Trader pub, and old warehouses now converted to new uses, are evocative of those busy times.

Following the granting of a charter in 1479, Tancred's successors created a thriving market town. The name Haverfordwest comes from the Old English haefer (a male goat) – this is where goats and sheep were driven through the river to market; the suffix 'west' was added in 1394 to avoid confusion with Hereford. From the time of James I, the mayor has carried the impressive title of Mayor and Admiral of the Port. He is assisted by a Sheriff, a role also preserved in Carmarthen. Haverfordwest's status was such that it had its own Member of Parliament until 1885.

It was the arrival of the railway that brought the river trade to an end, but Haverfordwest has maintained its position as an important commercial and administrative centre serving the county. The pleasing location, from the hill to the riverside, is graced by a collection of handsome buildings that give Haverfordwest one of the most charming townscapes in Wales.

The weir forms the upper limit of the tidal river. Two stone bridges cross the Cleddau at Haverfordwest. The Old Bridge was a gift in 1726 from Sir John Philipps of Picton Castle; it replaced the ford after which the town is named. The New Bridge was designed by William Owen in 1836, as part of a new approach to the town along Victoria Place.

The Riverside Shopping Centre is a pedestrianised area near to car parks and the bus station. The Riverside Market houses a group of shops selling gifts, books, toys and models, clocks and pet supplies; it also has a café on stilts over the river. A farmers' market does a brisk trade every other Friday along the quay and there are occasional French markets during the summer.

BISLEY H MUNT

43   **43**

ESTABLISHED 1796

PAINT YOUR OWN POTTERY

22

Paint your own Pottery

Coffee ~ Tea
Fresh Baguettes
Sandwiches
Salads

Above: The magnificent Shire Hall is a symmetrical, neo-classical building of great poise. Designed by William Owen and built in 1837, it stands on the site of a Quaker Meeting House which was relocated to the New Quay. It was a venue for Magistrates', County and Assize courts; it now houses the Black Sheep restaurant.

Left: As well as having many attractions of its own, Haverfordwest is an ideal and central base for touring Pembrokeshire, including the Pembrokeshire Coast National Park and the Preseli hills.

Opposite: This is another of those towns where a prosperous surrounding region supports a thriving selection of individually owned shops; Pembrokeshire even has an independent department store, Ocky White's.

Hay-on-Wye

Hay-on-Wye is some fifteen miles north-east of Brecon and twenty miles west of Hereford, along the A438. The most spectacular approach is the narrow and winding road from Llanvihangel Crucorney (on the A465, north-east of Abergavenny) past Llanthony Priory. Hay-on-Wye has a population of 1,469.

Market day
Thursday

This is quintessential border country; the agricultural richness of the lowlands surrounding Hay-on-Wye is plain to see. The name Hay derives from the Old English *haeg* and Norman French *haie*, meaning a fenced or hedged-in area of forest set aside for hunting. The Welsh name Gelli Gandryll suggests a grove or woodland that may have been divided into many small portions after being cleared.

Hay-on-Wye grew around bridging points over the river Wye and the Dulais Brook, the former being the county boundary between Brecknockshire and Radnorshire and the latter the border between England and Wales. From Hay Bluff, which rises to height of 2,227 feet to the south of the town, there are spectacular views of the Black Mountains, the Brecon Beacons, the green hills of Radnorshire and the lowlands of Herefordshire.

As one would expect from its border location, the site of Hay Castle has seen many battles. It was built by the infamous William de Breos, one of the most treacherous of the Marcher Lords, who was attacked with equal vigour from both sides of the border. The castle was destroyed by King John in 1216 and, it is said, was rebuilt in one night by William's wife, Maude de St Valery, who carried the stones in her apron. The castle was subsequently destroyed by Prince Llywelyn ap Iorwerth, rebuilt by Henry III, attacked by Simon de Montfort, captured by Edward II and destroyed by fire during Owain Glyndŵr's rebellion.

Hay-on-Wye is known as The Town of Books, thanks to the initiative of Richard Booth MBE – the self-proclaimed King of Hay and owner of Hay Castle. He opened a shop selling second-hand books here in 1961 and set the little town on course to become the largest centre for antiquarian and second-hand books in the world. The idea of a book town has since been exported to several countries. Hay is twinned with Timbuktu, a World Heritage Site and ancient seat of learning which is home to a large collection of medieval Islamic manuscripts.

The region is a paradise for walkers and cyclists. Hay stands at the junction of the Offa's Dyke National Trail and The Wye Valley Walk, a long-distance path that follows the river Wye from its source on Plynlimon, in the Cambrian Mountains, to its estuary at Chepstow.

At the end of May each year, the town fills to overflowing with eager bookworms attending the Hay Festival of Literature. Founded in 1988 by Norman Florence and his son Peter, who was formerly an actor, this has become (in the considered opinion of The New York Times) 'the most prestigious festival in the English-speaking world'. Famous writers, politicians (including Bill Clinton and Mikhail Gorbachev), poets, musicians and comedians provide a rich banquet of entertainment and 'brain food' during the ten days of the event.

The castle site, including the Jacobean mansion within the Norman walls, was acquired and restored by Richard Booth and now incorporates the largest of Hay's bookshops.

Hay's medieval maze of narrow streets has more than thirty bookshops, with a combined stock of more than a million books covering every conceivable subject – travel, history, biography, crime, children's books and so on.

Opposite: Thursday is Market Day and a strong selection of traders gather in Memorial Square, the old Butter Market and around the Town Clock, from 8am until mid afternoon. Food features strongly – fruit, vegetables, meat, fish, game, pies, cakes and preserves – but you are also likely to find garden plants, antiques, bric-a-brac and gifts. The popularity of the Town of Books has attracted many businesses other than bookshops. There are shops selling outdoor gear for those heading for the hills, along with a spectrum of art galleries, craft workshops, gift shops and antiques dealers. The gentleman with the magnificent beard is Karl Showler, one of the great characters of Hay-on-Wye. Seen here on volunteer duty at a charity stall in the Butter Market, he is also an internationally respected authority on bee-keeping.

Above: Hay's place as a bustling market town to which people travelled to shop for their needs was consolidated when, in 1816, the first horse-drawn tram linked the town with Brecon and intermediate stops. The tram was superseded in 1864 by the steam railway, which ran as far as Hereford and remained open until 1963. The river Wye was navigable for barges, there are records of a boatyard here, and in 1740 a bell for St Mary's church was brought upriver from the foundry in Chepstow.

Lampeter

Lampeter is in southern Ceredigion, close to the county border with Carmarthenshire, about twenty miles north-west of Llandovery. The coast, at Aberaeron, is twelve miles away. Lampeter has a population of 2,894.

Market days
Farmers' Market, every other Friday

Lampeter grew at the nodal point of five valleys: the Teifi, Dulas, Creuddyn, Eiddig and Hathren. There are several fortified farms from the Iron Age in the vicinity, during their later history their Celtic inhabitants lived, at varying degrees of peace or otherwise, alongside the Romans. The Roman road of Sarn Helen passes close by on its way from Carmarthen, past the gold mines at Dolau Cothi, and onward to the Roman bases of Segontium (Caernarfon) and Caerhun (Conwy).

The small Norman motte of Stephen's Castle stands in the grounds of Lampeter University. It's fortifications were destroyed by Welsh forces in 1137. Another motte known as Bigod's Castle is just outside the town. These guarded small settlements that faded into obscurity; the later growth of the town was driven by the commercial needs of its hinterland. The English name Lampeter is a corruption of Llanbedr meaning Church of St Peter. The Welsh name adds Pont Steffan, recognising that the bridge was guarded by Stephen's Castle.

Lampeter was granted the right to hold a market in 1285 and until the eighteenth century remained a small settlement gathered around St Peter's Church. It was in the nineteenth century that the town found its true vocation, as a centre of learning. The Grammar School was established in 1805 (and chosen by Sir Walter Scott for his son's education), followed by St David's College in 1822. Within the UK, only Oxford and Cambridge universities are older.

The support of the Harford family, owners of the nearby Falcondale estate, was instrumental in the development of the college and the growth of the town. A more urban layout, including Market Street, College Street and Bridge Street, gradually took shape during the second half of the nineteenth century. With the elevation of the college into the University of Wales, Lampeter became (and remains) the smallest university town in the UK.

Ceredigion is another of the prime farming regions of Wales, as is clear from the green and fertile countryside around Lampeter. The Derry Ormond Tower, in the distance, is said to have been built by unemployed workers as a folly for the squire David J Morgan.

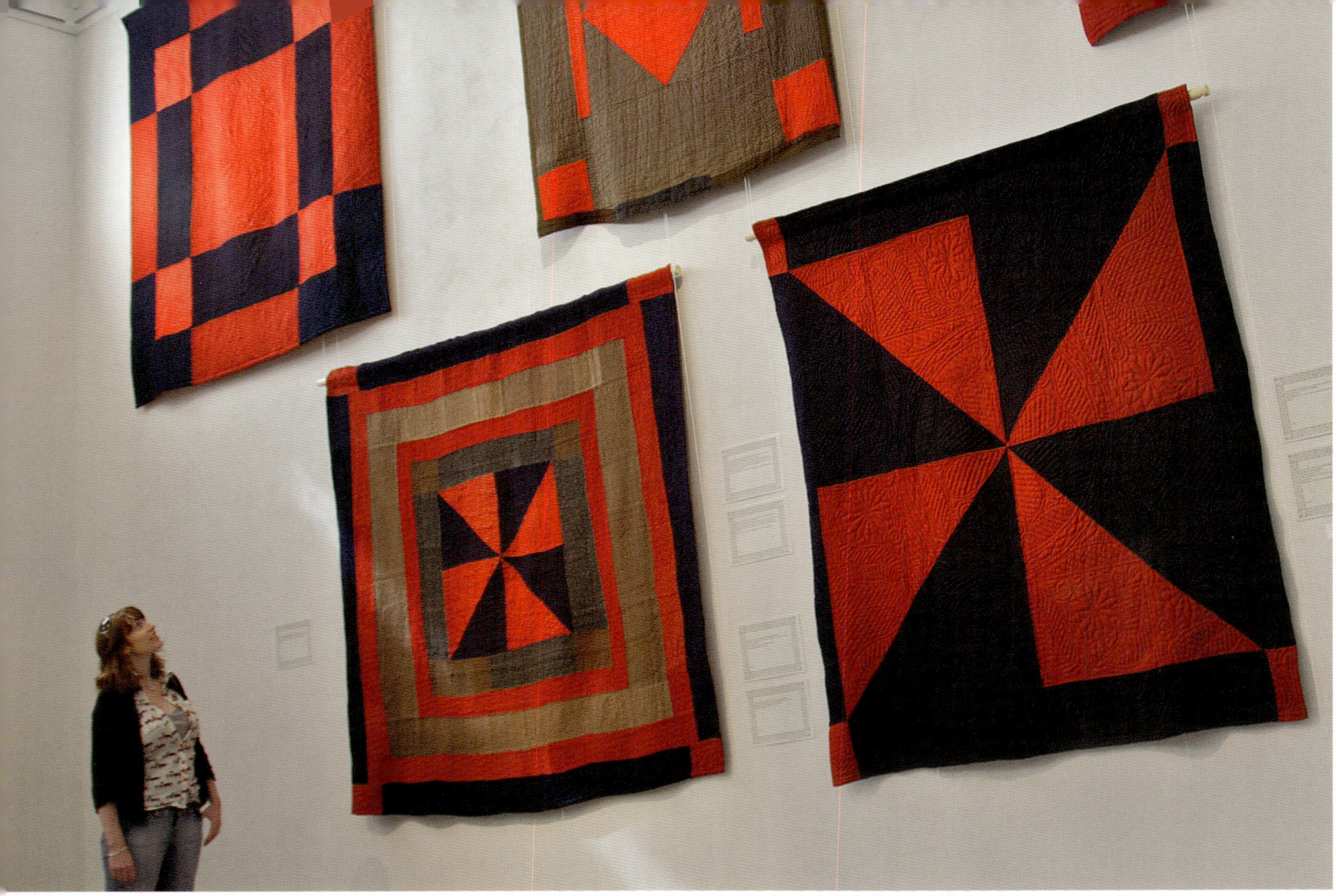

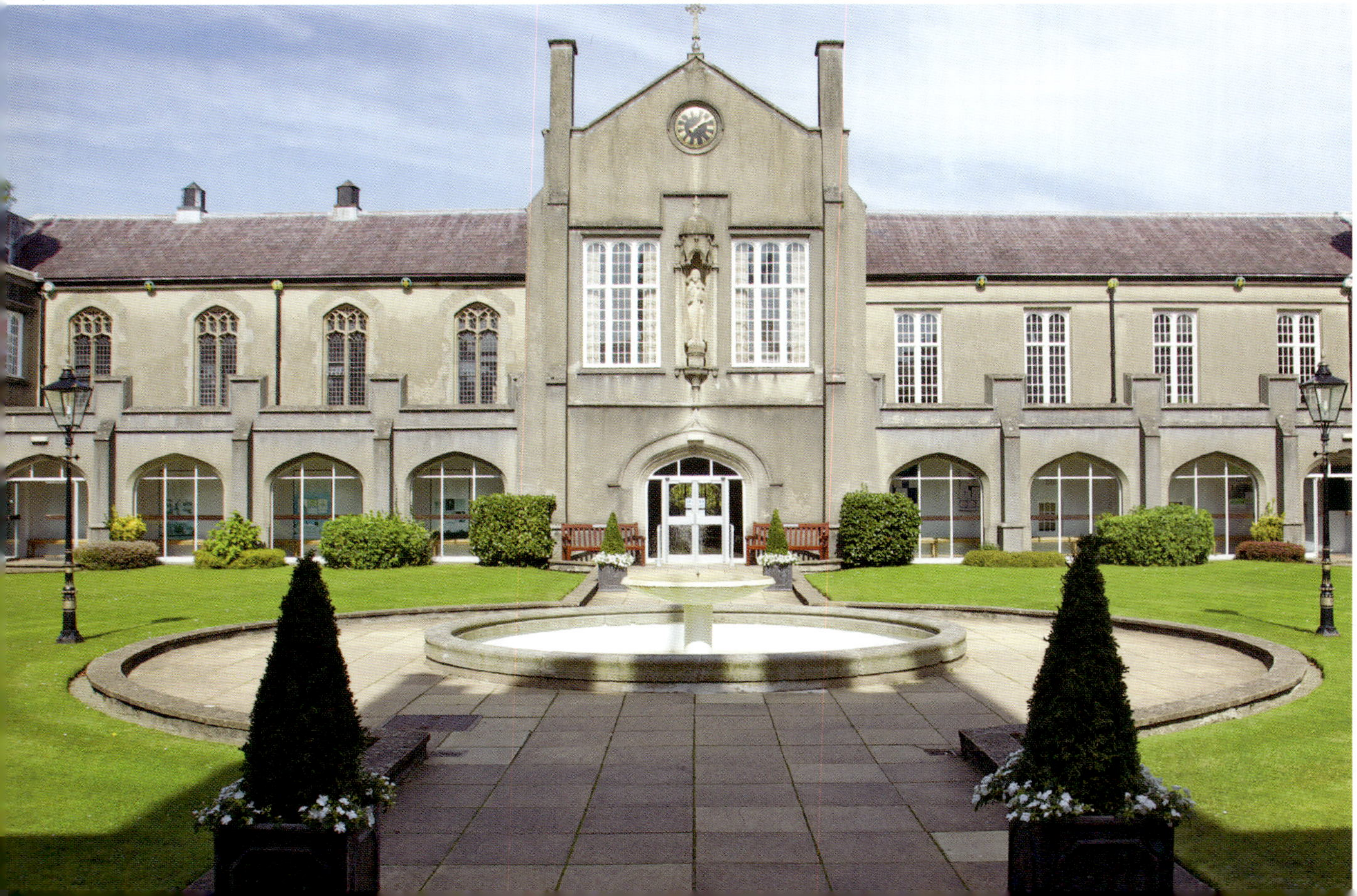

Above: The Falcondale Hotel, above the town, has fourteen acres of magnificent grounds, famous for their rhododendrons and azaleas.

Left: The immaculately maintained war memorial commemorates local men who served their country.

Opposite above: The Town Hall houses the Jen Jones Welsh Quilts Centre, where you may learn all about these practical and colourful examples of folk art.

Opposite below: Lampeter University has an attractive Oxbridge-style courtyard. Upwards of a thousand students significantly increase the population of the town during term time.

Lampeter has several independently owned outfitters that are more than able to kit out the gentlemen and ladies of Ceredigion and Carmarthenshire for the more smart and formal occasions. There's also a good selection of more practically inclined shops, including an excellent ironmonger's and tool shop, and many pubs and restaurants.

Opposite: The solid and symmetrical Town Hall reflects Lampeter's growth in Victorian times, and the need for a meeting place for the council. The Mayor remains a popular figure; civic pride is expressed in floral displays that bring colour to the streets every summer.

Llandeilo

Llandeilo grew where the river Tywi emerges from the hills to meander across the lowlands of south Carmarthenshire to its estuary. One of several market towns along the A40, it is also conveniently linked via the A483 to the western end of the M4 motorway. Llandeilo has a population of 1,731.

Market day
Friday

The town sits strategically on a hill, sufficiently high above the river to be safe from flooding. The graceful stone bridge dates from 1848; it was, at the time, one of the longest single-arched bridges in Britain.

During the sixth century or the Age of Saints – this part of the Tywi valley was brought to prominence by Saint Teilo, a contemporary of St David. He established a clas – an ecclesiastical settlement populated by monks, with himself as Abbot – which evolved into one of the most important centres of Celtic Christianity. The present church is mainly Victorian, built in the late 1840s, though the tower is from the thirteenth century.

Dinefwr Castle, a mile or so outside the town, was the seat of the rulers of Deheubarth, the south-western kingdom of early-medieval Wales. It was the residence in the ninth century of Rhodri Mawr, one of the greatest of all Welsh kings; in the tenth century of Hywel Dda (Hywel the Good), who formulated an enlightened body of law for Wales; and in the twelfth century of Lord Rhys, who led the Welsh resistance against the Normans.

After Edward I's army of eight hundred knights and fifteen thousand foot soldiers swept through Wales in 1277, an English plantation borough called Newton was founded at Dinefwr. The Rice family, or Barons Dynevor, later built the mansion Newton House, which (along with the whole of Dinefwr Park) is now in the care of the National Trust. Archaeologists have discovered the foundations of two Roman forts in the park, one of which is second in size in Wales only to the legionary fortress at Caerleon.

Llandeilo became an important market town, with a charter to hold a weekly market and three annual fairs. In 1401, in a sort of back-handed compliment that recognised its strategic importance, Llandeilo was attacked and largely burned to the ground by Owain Glyndŵr. During the more peaceful times that followed, the town acquired its present mix of architecture; much of the main street, Rhosmaen Street, with its ornamented shop fronts – is Victorian.

On a perfect summer's day, it is possible to compare this part of the Tywi valley to one of the more verdant regions around the Mediterranean. Perhaps this was some consolation to the Roman officers posted here to guard the route taken by the gold they mined at Dolau Cothi, a few miles away, to the Imperial Mint at Lyon.

Left and overleaf: The town has been the subject of a co-ordinated effort to beat the decline of many a High Street, in the face of out-of-town supermarkets and megastores, by encouraging the establishment of upmarket shops.

St Teilo's original clas became the mother church of the region. It owned a beautifully illuminated book of the Gospels, in Latin, said to have been presented by a local man who had bought it 'for the price of a good horse'. Its margins and blank pages are dotted with notes and lists of the community's possessions, some of which are the earliest surviving examples of written Welsh. Towards the end of the eleventh century, the book was removed to Lichfield Cathedral where, except for a short time during the Civil Wars, it has remained.

127 GOLDSMITHS N.WALL SILVERSMITHS 36

BB
Beauty Salon   Aromatherapy

The BOOKSHOP Llandeilo   Tel 01558 823040

New, Used &
Antiquarian Books
Prints & Pictures

BOOKSHOP

BOOKSHOP

OPEN NOW!

FRESH FRUIT & VEG
TOWY STORES
01558 824000
FRESH LOCAL STRAWBERRIES

Cigydd teuluol
HUGH EVANS & SON
Family butcher
COTTAGE PIE
£1.89

Above: John Wesley preached in Llandeilo; he held the town's first Methodist meetings at the Bear Inn, now the Cawdor Hotel, during the 1760s. The old Public Hall and Literary Institute occupied the former Calvinist Methodist Chapel, built in 1788.

Left: Llandeilo's wool shop is especially well stocked.

Opposite: The former National School, above the town, was built in the 1850s by the renowned London architect William Teulon on behalf of Lord Dynevor. It has some fine Gothic Revival detailing including some fierce-looking gargoyles. The half-timbered porch, next door to the schoolroom, was the entrance to the schoolmaster's house.

Llandovery

Llandovery sits comfortably on the floor of the Tywi valley, a little over twenty miles west of Brecon along the A40, where it meets the A483 from Builth Wells, and half-an-hour or so northward from the M4 motorway. It was an important meeting point for the drovers' roads that once criss-crossed the region. The town has a railway station. Llandovery has a population of 2,235.

Market day
Farmers' Market, last Saturday of each month

In 1854, George Borrow, in his book Wild Wales, wrote: "Llandovery is a small but beautiful town situated among fertile meadows. It is a water-girded spot, whence its name, Llandovery or Llanymddyfri which signifies 'the church surrounded by water'."

Bounded by the rivers Brân, Gwydderig and Tywi (and with the river Bawddwr running in culverts beneath the town), it is indeed an attractive place – especially the unusually colourful and picturesque central square with its Toytown proportions. But it also has solid significance in the history of Welsh culture, as the home of several major literary figures.

The Tonn Press, established by William and David Rees, performed a valuable role during the mid-nineteenth century in editing and printing important works. These included the popular collection of inspirational poems 'Canwyll y Cymry' (The Welshman's Candle) by local vicar Rhys Prichard; the English translation of the medieval legends, The Mabinogion, by Lady Charlotte Guest; and the herbal remedies of the Physicians of Myddfai, as remembered and used by local people. William Rees also served as Town Clerk and was instrumental in bringing the railway to Llandovery.

William Williams (1717-91) is legendary in Wales as an early leader of the Methodist movement and as the nation's most prolific and best-loved hymn writer. The words of many of his hymns may fairly be described as poetry of a high order. His descendants still live at his home, Pantycelyn farm, outside Llandovery.

The town has a Mayor and the civic silverware includes two fine maces made during the reign of Charles I, which are carried before the Mayor during civic events. The present Sergeants-at-Mace, locally born brothers George and Les Adams, have a combined service in their posts of more than eighty years. Llandovery also has a Town Crier and, every other (odd-numbered) year, in July hosts a competition for the shrinking violets who are accomplished in this early form of public broadcasting.

Llandovery conveys a distinct feeling of being in western Wales, even before you hear the change of accent, as the uplands of the Brecon Beacons and The Black Mountain give way to the sheltered Vale of Tywi and the gentler landscapes of northern Carmarthenshire. The white tower to the left looks as if it belongs to a church, but is in fact Llandovery College, an independent boarding and day-school founded in 1847 by Thomas Phillips. Here the Welsh language and its culture are given a central place.

The almost unfeasibly quaint market square is still a place of commerce and activity though it is generally free of livestock, which is nowadays sold at the modern market beyond the castle. The continuing usefulness of the small town to the population of the surrounding countryside is reflected in the presence of the major high-street banks. The date of Llandovery's charter, 1485, is proudly displayed on the wall of the town hall.

Llandovery has relatively few shops, in comparison with the larger towns of the region and the metropolis of Swansea, less than an hour away. But there is something rather pleasing, in a low-stress kind of way, about buying fresh food and other basics from a local supplier. Gerwyn Williams of Llandeilo is a regular visitor with his fruit and vegetable stall. The future of the Post Office is a concern, as in small towns and villages throughout the UK. People value having a local branch as a place to make transactions and catch up on news, and look upon the postman as a valuable member of the community.

THE DROVERS
Bed and Breakfast
@
9 Market Square, Llandovery
★ ★ ★ ★
www.droversllandovery.co.uk
01550 721115

Llangefni

Llangefni is in the centre of Anglesey, just north of the A55 expressway. It is at the heart of the island's well-signed network of walking and cycling routes, which follow pleasant lanes and a former railway into attractive countryside. Llangefni has a population of 4,662.

Market days
Thursday and Saturday

Llangefni stands at the northern extremity of the Malltraeth marsh, which reaches far into Anglesey from its south-western coast. Before the early-nineteenth century, when this low-lying area was drained and protected by a sea wall, the combination of a high tide and heavy rain would cause flooding around the town square where the river Cefni flows by.

Plas Penmynydd, east of Llangefni, was the birthplace of Owen Tudor, a soldier and courtier who fought at Agincourt. Through his relationship with the young widow of Henry V, Catherine de Valois – whom he is believed to have secretly married – he became the grandfather of Henry VII, founder of the House of Tudor.

Llanerchymedd, a busy centre of shoemaking a little further north, was for centuries the site of Anglesey's largest market, but was overtaken by Llangefni during the late-eighteenth century. Llangefni became county town of Anglesey in 1889 – its size, rail access and commercial importance eclipsing the historical claim of Beaumaris. Nowadays Anglesey's main livestock market, which remains a vital engine of the rural economy, is to be found at the Gaerwen Industrial Estate a few miles away.

During the early-nineteenth century the leading preachers Christmas Evans (Baptist) and John Elias (Calvinist Methodist) ministered at chapels in Llangefni; they were 'superstars' of the era, drawing large crowds wherever they appeared. St Cyngar's church demonstrates remarkable continuity of worship: it contains the Culidorus Stone from the fifth century, a twelfth-century font, a sundial dated 1673 and a wooden chest (in which parish records were kept) from 1811.

Llangefni is a hard-working sort of town, catering for locals as much as for visitors. Both groups of people find much to see and enjoy at Oriel Ynys Môn, the museum and gallery where Anglesey's story may be explored and the work of its greatest artists seen.

St Cyngar's Church and the beginning of the nature trail through The Dingle.

Llangefni sits in a sheltered spot between two gentle ridges in the corrugated lowland of Anglesey. As county town and administrative centre for the island, it provides all the necessary functions: local government, police, schools, banks, shops, solicitors, doctors, dentists, opticians, churches, chapels, sports grounds and so on with a wide range of employment in its centre, industrial estate and business park.

THE MARKET

WARM
WELCOME

FOOD
SERVED
ALL DAY

GARDEN
AT REAR

CROESO
CYNNES

BWYD
AR GAEL
DRWY'R DYDD

GARDD
YN CEFN

Llangefni's town clock is the only Boer War memorial on Anglesey. It was built in memory of George Prichard Rayner of Tre Ysgawen Hall, north of the town, which is now a hotel. The most practical way of bringing the limestone from the quarry at Traeth Bychan, on the east coast of Anglesey, was to take it by ship to Llandudno – completely in the wrong direction – and then to convey it all the way back to Llangefni by rail.

Oriel Ynys Môn, on the outskirts of Llangefni, is Anglesey's main museum and art gallery. Its exhibitions chronicle the long and fascinating history of the island, from prehistoric times to the present day. The work of two of Anglesey's most eminent artists is prominent. Sir Kyffin Williams RA had a rare ability to convey the atmosphere of landscape, seascape, weather, light and the character of people in his trade-mark style of applying thick layers of paint with a palette knife. Charles Tunnicliffe OBE RA was one of the foremost wildlife artists of the twentieth century, a meticulous technician renowned for his superbly detailed, dimensionally accurate drawings and paintings of birds and animals. Oriel Ynys Môn also puts on an ever-changing progamme of exhibitions by local artists and has a well-stocked shop and an excellent café.

The Dingle nature reserve is a wooded valley, rich in wildlife and history, which extends into the heart of the town. A showpiece reclamation of an industrial site, it was the location of Llangefni's fulling mill, which was powered by the river Cefni where it rushes through a gorge made by glacial meltwater. Wooden boardwalks, suitable for walkers and wheelchairs, lead past sculptures of natural forms: the dragonfly stands near St Cyngar's Church and the split-oak trunks, a 'petrified forest', form the entrance at the old station. Heron, woodpecker, goldcrest, kingfisher and dipper are among the many species of birds to be seen and heard here. Carpets of bluebells make a wonderful sight in the springtime.

Llanidloes

Llanidloes is centrally located at the narrowest part of mid Wales, just off the A470 and approximately mid-way between Aberystwyth and the Wales-England border. It is no longer served by the railway (the station has been preserved and converted into offices) but is only a relatively short bus, taxi or cycle ride from stations at Newtown and Caersws. Llanidloes has a population of 2,807.

Market day
Saturday

There are many half-timbered buildings in the centre of Llanidloes, including several shops and some highly atmospheric pubs. The largest of all is the National Westminster Bank, on a corner opposite the Market Hall which was built as recently as 1926 in the Arts and Crafts timber-framed revival style, to fit in with the others.

Site of the monastic settlement of St Idloes, Llanidloes is in the ancient region of Arwystli, part of Powys, though at one stage it became a detached part of the diocese of Bangor. The question of whether Welsh or English law should determine its ownership was a bone of contention during the 1280s and contributed to the breakdown in relations between Prince Llywelyn ap Gruffudd and Edward I. The town received its charter in 1280 and a market has been held there ever since.

During the first half of the nineteenth century, Llanidloes was rather larger than it is today having, at its peak, a population approaching four thousand. Many people were employed in the woollen industry and its related trades; thirty flannel manufacturers were recorded in a trade directory of Llanidloes in 1835. Additionally lead was mined in the surrounding hills, the smelting of which brought additional work and prosperity to the town.

For the textile workers and miners, however, wages were low and living conditions were harsh. In 1839, several issues of concern – poor pay, inadequate housing, the injustices of the Poor Law Amendment Act of 1834 (which had introduced the much-hated workhouses) and the publication of The People's Charter by the Chartists in 1838 – sparked the disenchantment of the exploited workers into protest on the streets of Llanidloes.

The Chartists, also active elsewhere in Wales, sought greater civic and political rights for ordinary people. Their leaders in Wales were largely from a Methodist, chapel background and emphasised the need for non-violent protest. However, Llanidloes achieved national fame when the mainly peaceful demonstrations, blown somewhat out of proportion by influential local figures, were vigorously repressed. In a quite disproportionate response, the town was placed under military occupation for a year and some of the protesters were transported to Australia.

Historically, the rivers of Wales – Severn, Wye, Usk, Tywi, Teifi, Dyfi, Mawddach, Conwy, Dee and others – have provided sheltered, valley-floor locations suitable for settlement and, eventually, for development into market towns with good access in several directions. Llanidloes, in its cosy setting at the confluence of the rivers Severn and Clywedog, surrounded by gentle hills, shows this clearly.

The Town Hall dominates the wide and pleasant thoroughfare of Great Oak Street. The Trewython Arms, which stands opposite, was the focal point of the Chartist uprising of 1839. A crowd stormed the building and released two of their number who had been detained by special constables sent from London.

The timber-framed Old Market Hall, the only one of its kind remaining in Wales, is at the heart of the town. It contains an exhibition about this form of construction, which is characteristic of this border region of the Severn valley. Tree-ring dating shows that it was built between 1612 and 1622. Some of the timbers are older than that and were probably recycled from an earlier market hall. It was originally known as the Booth Hall, from the booths or stalls congregated under and around it. An upstairs room served as a Court of Law and a meeting place for Quakers, Baptists and Methodists; it later became a store for wool flannel and then a Working Men's Institute. The building remained in use as a market until the early-twentieth century and housed the Llanidloes Museum from 1933 until 1995.

Above: John Wesley preached from this stone at the north-western corner of the Market Hall.

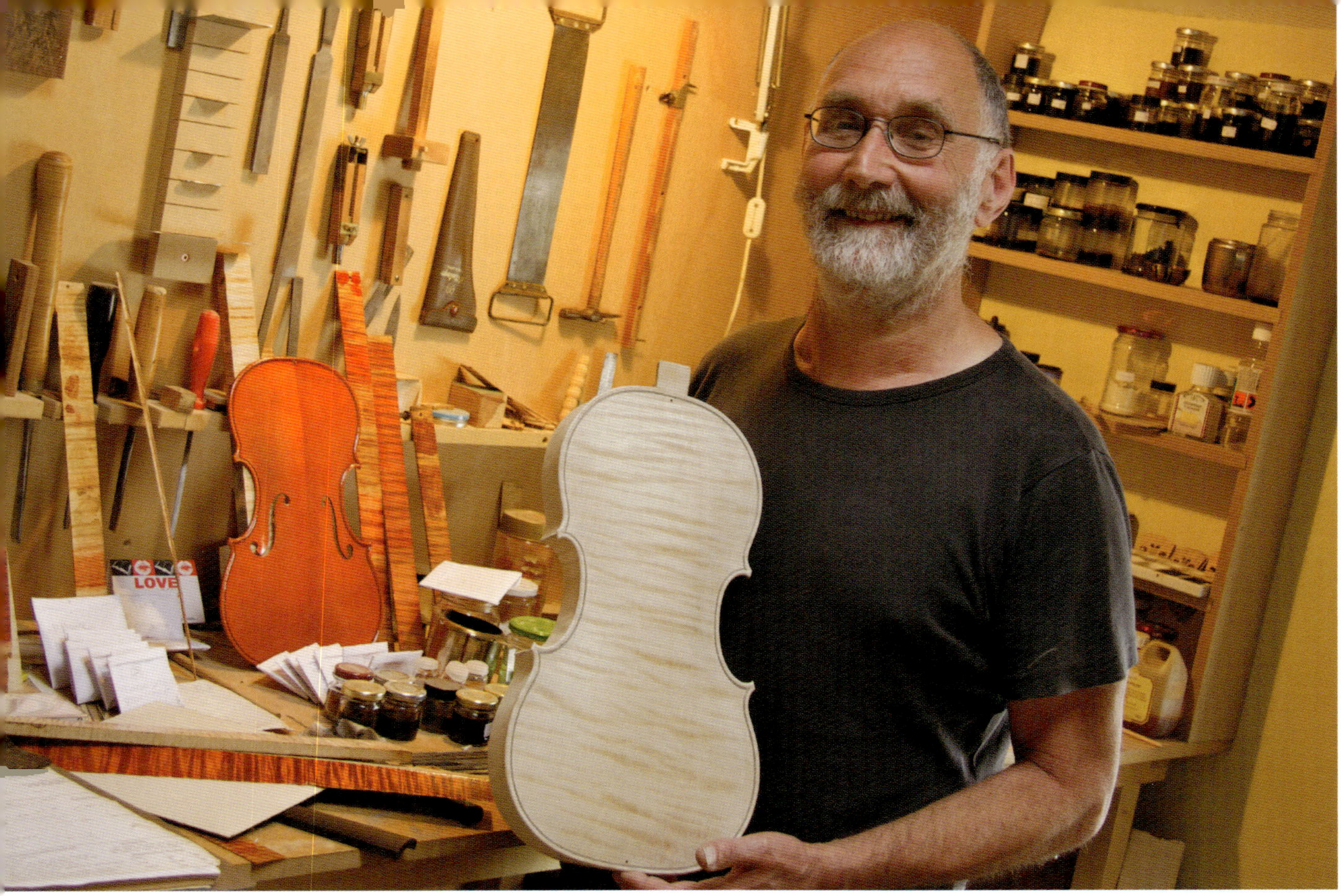
LOVE

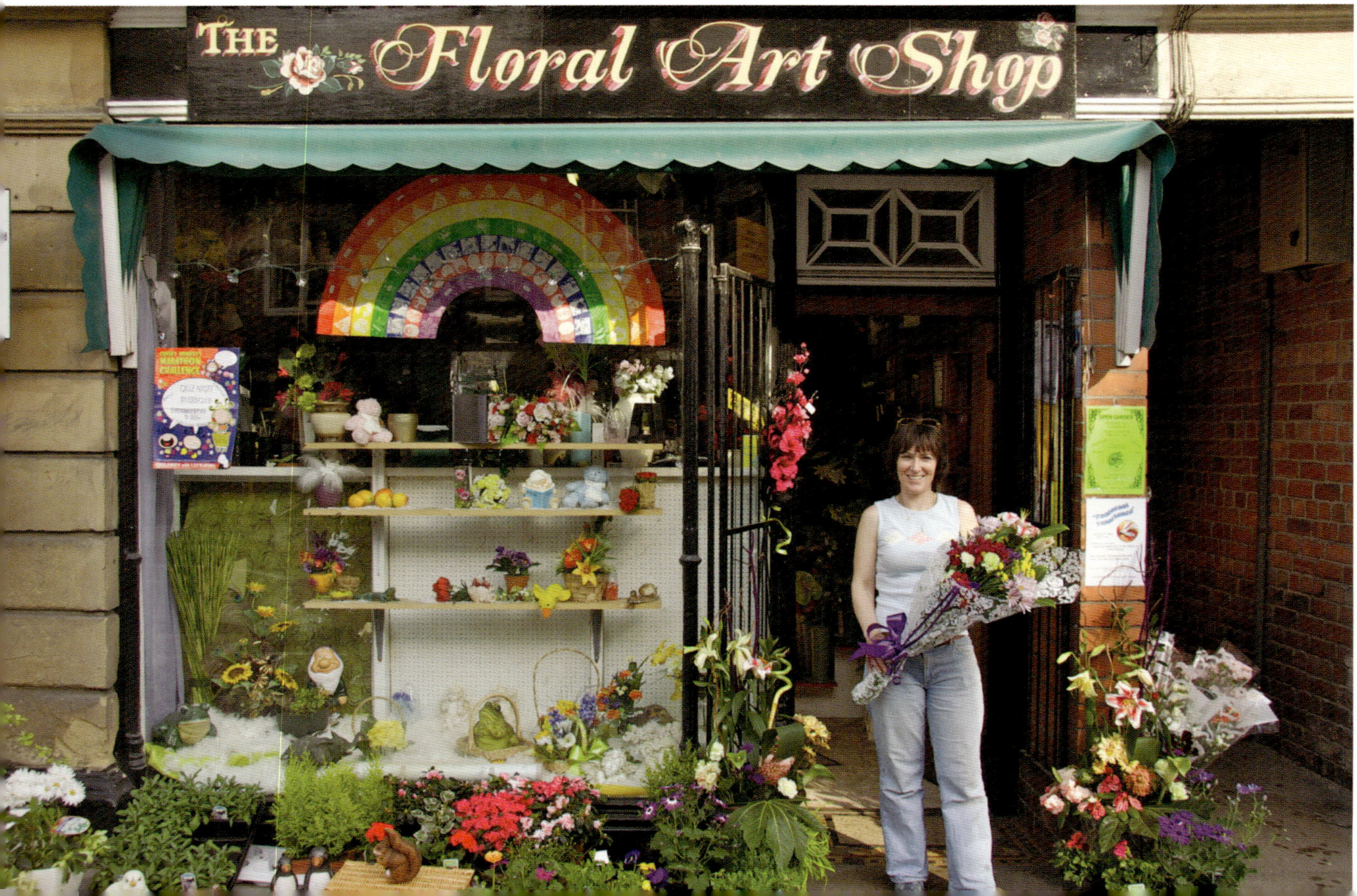
THE Floral Art Shop

Opposite: There's a great variety of shops in the town and a small market is held in the Town Hall every Saturday. At Compton's Yard, off Great Oak Street, a charitable trust provides premises for environmentally aware organisations and businesses ranging from the UK office of the Forest Stewardship Council to the Great Oak vegetarian café and the workshop of Peter Croll, violin maker.

Above: The prosperity generated by the wool trade is still evident in the fabric of the town today. The details of construction and decoration don't exactly give the impression that the buildings were thrown together on a shoestring budget. There are several chapels of the finest stonemasonry, handsome business premises and homes distinguished by decorative features of great style. The red doorway, framed between green pillars, is that of Castle House, dating from 1789.

Llanrwst

Llanrwst is on the A470, eleven miles south of the A55 expressway and four miles north of Betws-y-Coed. It is also on the railway line that runs from Llandudno Junction to Betws-y-Coed and onward to Blaenau Ffestiniog, one of the most scenic rail journeys in the UK. Llanrwst has a population of 3,037.

Market day
Tuesday

The streets around Ancaster Square are characterised by substantial buildings including coaching inns, merchants' houses and banks that proclaim their dependability through their solid architecture.

Here, as elsewhere, the ability to cross the river was the deciding factor in establishing a settlement. Llanrwst was the lowest bridging point on the river Conwy until Thomas Telford built his suspension bridge near Conwy Castle in 1826. There may have been a small harbour here since Roman times; the tidal estuary was navigable for small craft. An alleyway, Steam Packet Lane, once led to a small boatyard on the river bank.

Llanrwst has seen much conflict: at the time of the Normans, during Owain Glyndŵr's campaigns and during the Wars of the Roses. It was declared a 'free borough' by Prince Llywelyn ap Gruffudd, in defiance of Edward I and the Bishop of St Asaph, and continues to claim independence. The town has its own flag and the council has even applied, unsuccessfully, for a seat at the United Nations!

In more peaceful times a wide range of trades became established: brewers, tanners, dyers, soap makers, carpenters, coopers, wheelwrights, farriers, blacksmiths and others. During the eighteenth century, Llanrwst was especially renowned for its clockmakers and harpmakers, the former being easily recognisable by their habit of wearing top hats to advertise their status as skilled craftsmen. John Richard, harpist to Queen Charlotte, was born at the King's Head tavern in 1711.

The central square, Ancaster Square, is named after the Duke of Ancaster, who married Mary Wynn of nearby Gwydir Castle. Llanrwst's Town Hall was demolished in 1962, it was crowned by an eighteenth-century 'birdcage' clock made by John Owen, founder of the town's clock industry. Its mechanism may be seen in the fascinating Almshouses Museum, just off the square, which tells the story of the town in rooms themed to the seventeenth and nineteenth centuries and on to the 1940s.

The verdant Conwy valley is another prime agricultural region. Cattle and crops are farmed on the valley floor, with sheep predominating on the higher land to both sides. It's a captivating place at any time of year, but perhaps especially so on a bright spring day, with new leaves emerging and cloud shadows racing across the landscape. The parish church of St Grwst may be seen in the centre of the picture, at the edge of the town, on the river bank.

Inigo Jones Bridge. The design of the elegant stone bridge over the river Conwy (built around 1636) is often attributed to the great architect Inigo Jones, though there is no conclusive evidence of this. Driving across it requires care; its hump is so steep that oncoming cars cannot be seen until the last second – whoever is first to the middle wins! The sundial commemorates the tricentenary of the bridge. The creeper-covered house, Ty Hwnt i'r Bont (once a courthouse) is now a National Trust tearoom; it contains dramatic pictures of the river in flood.

The history of Gwydir Castle, ancestral home of the Wynn family, is closely linked with that of the town, which it overlooks from the other side of the river. John Leland – the antiquary employed by Henry VIII to retrieve valuable documents from the monasteries, on dissolution – wrote in 1536: 'Gwydir lieth two bowshots above the river Conwy; it is a pretty place'. It is famous both for the peacocks that stalk its grounds and for the ghosts reputed to haunt its corridors. The surviving building dates from around 1500 with numerous alterations; the present owners have done a wonderful job of restoring the house and gardens in authentic fashion.

OWAIN
TYWYSOG CYMRU
PRINCE OF WALES
GLYNDŴR

Owain, tydi yw'n dyhead - Owain,
Ti piau'n harddeliad,
Piau'r her yn ein parhad
A ffrewyll ein deffroad.

Machynlleth

Machynlleth is at the north-western corner of Powys, near the border with Gwynedd, approximately mid-way between Aberystwyth and Dolgellau. It is linked by rail to Aberystwyth and Shrewsbury – and, via the Cambrian Coast line, to Pwllheli. It is a gateway to southern Snowdonia. Machynlleth has a population of 2,147.

Market day
Wednesday

This monument to Owain Glyndŵr stands in the grounds of Plas Machynlleth, former home of the Londonderry family. A dark-stone building on Maengwyn Street is said to be the location of Owain Glyndŵr's parliament, to which he invited Welsh regional leaders and representatives from Scotland, France and Spain. The Grade 1 listed building is certainly medieval, but it appears to date from later than 1404, when Owain convened his parliament. The Owain Glyndŵr Institute, next door, opened in 1912 and houses an exhibition about the charismatic leader.

There are the usual Roman and Norman remains hereabouts but Machynlleth was put properly on the map in the thirteenth century. A charter granted to Owen de la Pole, Lord of Powys, in 1291 gave rights to hold 'a market at Machynlleth every Wednesday for ever and two fairs every year'.

Machynlleth is where Owain Glyndŵr held his Parliament in 1404. He was the last leader to succeed in unifying Wales, in the hope of creating an independent nation, but his rebellion was put down by Henry IV. In 1485 Henry Tudor, another Welshman, became King Henry VII of England, following his victory at Bosworth Field. His son, Henry VIII, passed the Acts of Union by which Wales became part of the United Kingdom.

The region around Machynlleth is rich in minerals. Slate – much in demand for roofing the nation – was quarried at Corris to the north and lead was mined in the hills to the south-east, at Dylife. In 1859, a tramroad for horse-drawn trucks from Corris was built through Machynlleth to Derwenlas, the head of navigation on the river Dyfi, two miles west of the town.

The town's fortunes were given an enormous boost when the steam railway arrived in 1863. Machynlleth became an important depot and junction, with many people employed on the railway. However improved transport did lessen the need for small towns to be self-sufficient in their shops and tradesmen such as blacksmiths, coopers, tanners, tailors, shoemakers, milliners, clockmakers and others, as it became easier to visit the larger centres.

In recent times, though, artists and designer-makers have made a reappearance and Machynlleth has a cluster of shops and workshops whose owners and suppliers produce a wide range of appealing items of high quality. The Spectrum Gallery and the shop at the Museum of Modern Art, Wales, are good places to start.

The combined effects of glaciation and the river Dyfi have created a wide valley in a landscape of gentle hills, which is good news in terms of ease of communication in several directions. The sea is just a few miles to the west, so the climate is generally spared the extremes found further inland. The Glyndŵr Way National Trail passes through the area.

Above: Maengwyn Street, the main street, is named after these two white stones, clearly once a single pillar. These were likely to have been a pre-Roman direction stone or 'signpost' – these were routinely smashed during later centuries because of their perceived pagan connections. There are records of the street as far back as the sixteenth century, so the stones have certainly been here for more than five hundred years.

Right: Some attribute these ancient steps to the Romans, who mined minerals locally and had a small fort on the hill to which the steps lead. Others believe they were made for farmers bringing their sheep to market.

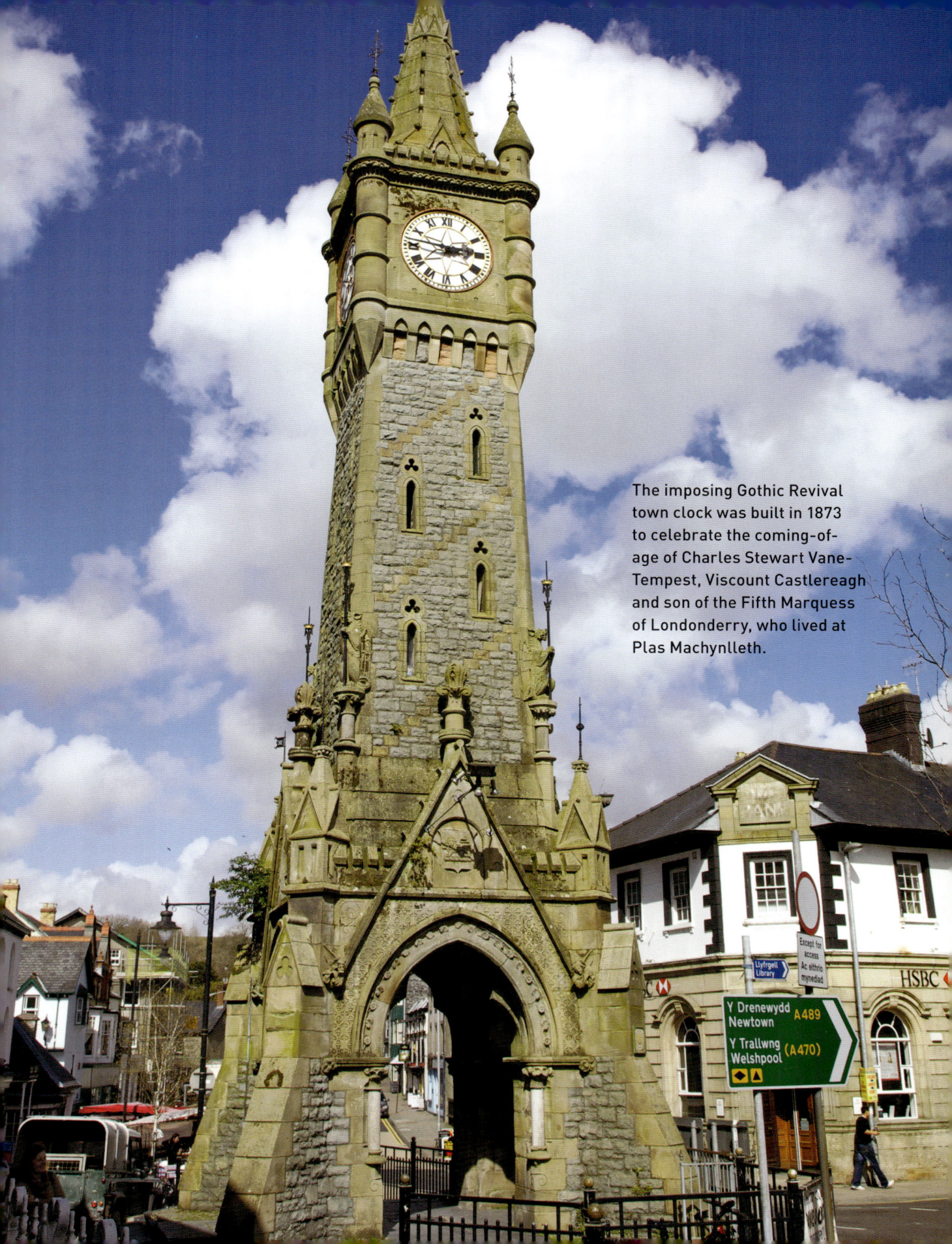

The imposing Gothic Revival town clock was built in 1873 to celebrate the coming-of-age of Charles Stewart Vane-Tempest, Viscount Castlereagh and son of the Fifth Marquess of Londonderry, who lived at Plas Machynlleth.

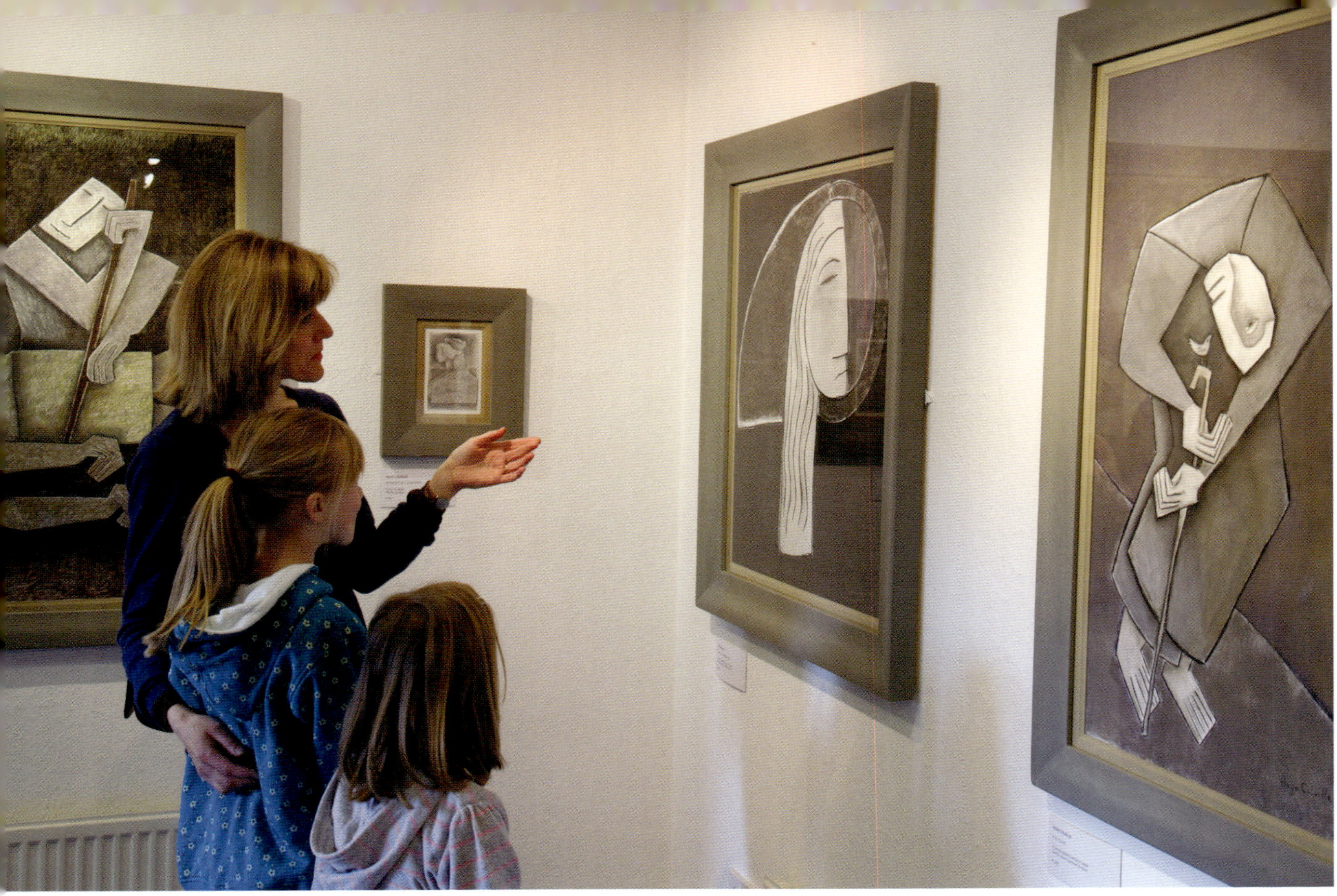

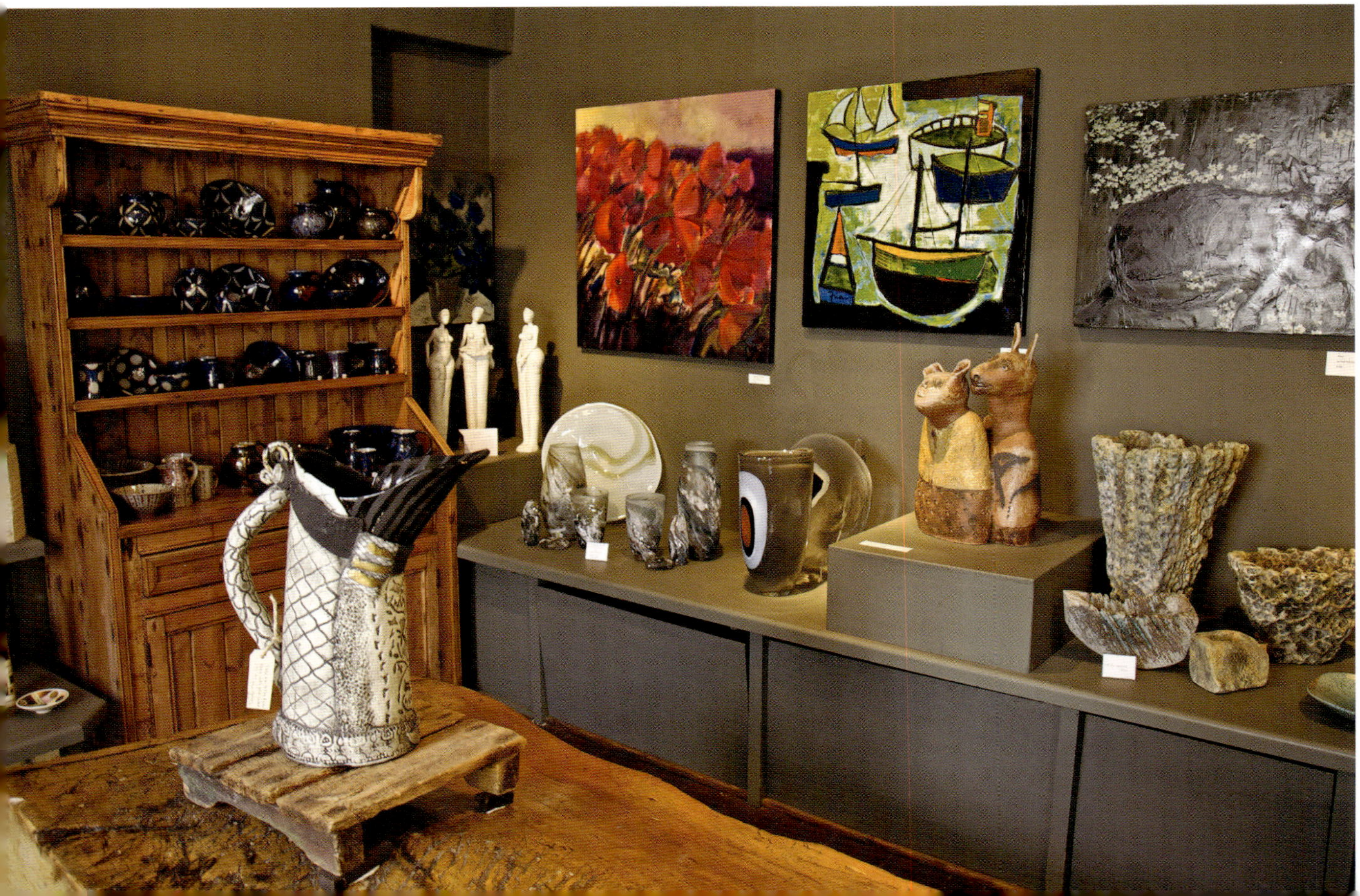

Machynlleth is an exceedingly agreeable place in which to shop – the national retail chains are nowhere to be seen! The outdoor market is still going strong and the shops are low-stress environments in which to browse. The Centre for Alternative Technology is just up the road at Corris, and several shops in Machynlleth reflect environmental priorities.

Opposite top: The former Wesleyan Methodist chapel, Y Tabernacl, is now the Museum of Modern Art, Wales. It has a regularly changing programme of exhibitions and is also the main venue for the annual Machynlleth Festival, a feast of quality music.

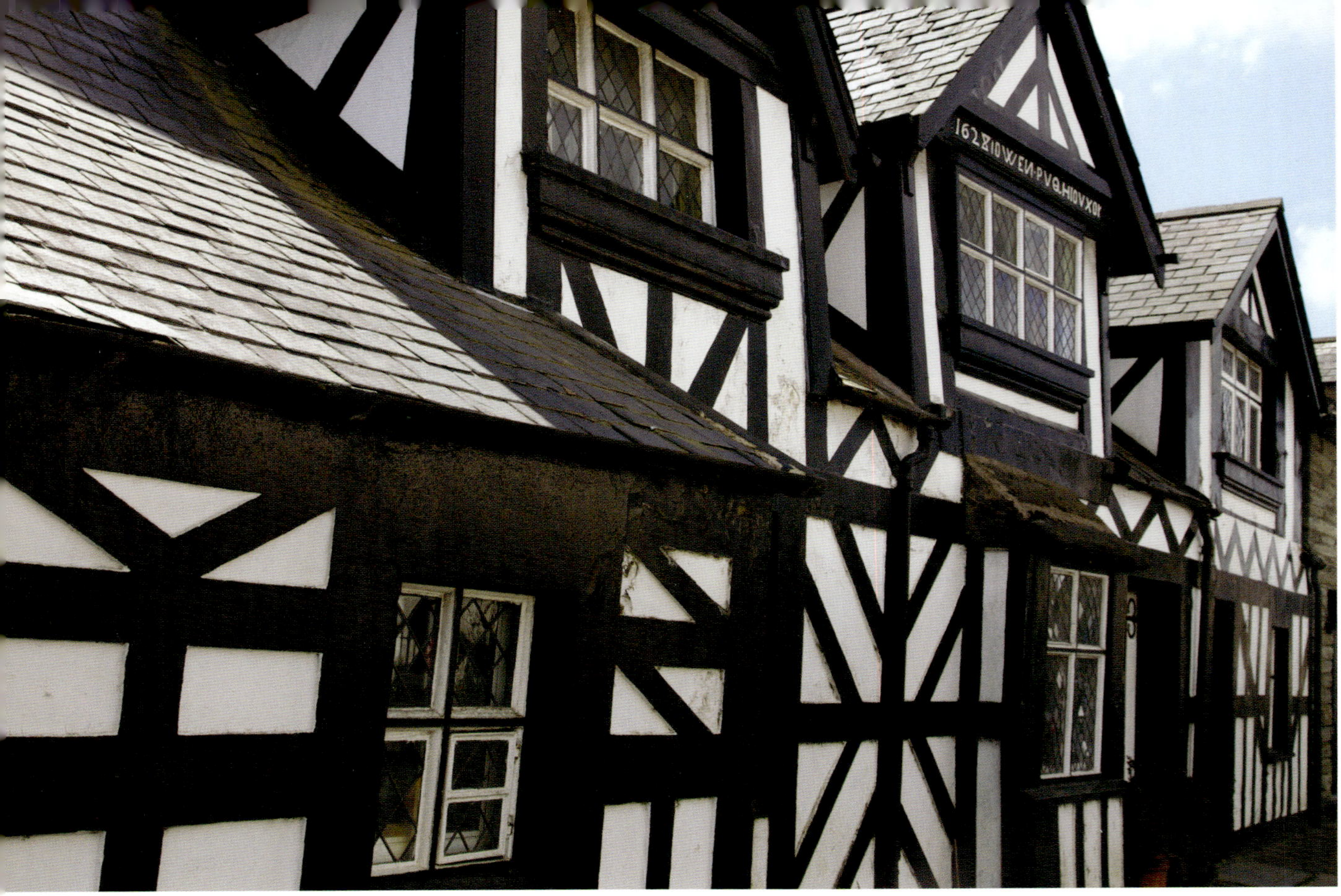
1628 IOWEN·PVGH

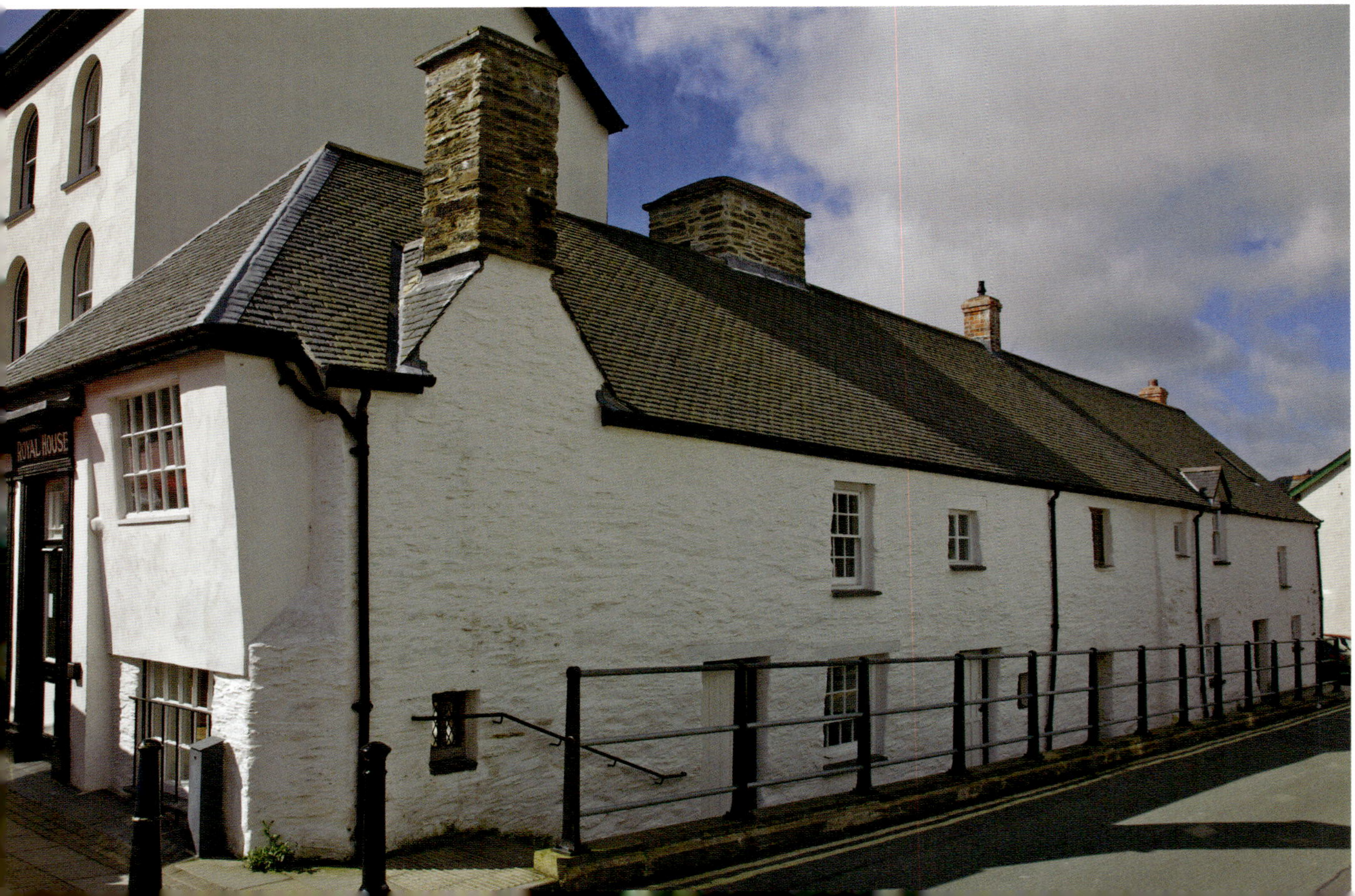
ROYAL HOUSE

The town's stock of buildings is highly varied, in both date and style. The whitewashed building – Royal House, on Penrallt Street – is a reputed resting place of Henry Tudor on his way to Bosworth Field, and of Charles I on his way to Chester in 1643. The Almshouses (above) with their attractive gardens were built by the same family. The solid building with the horseshoe-shaped door is, of course, the old smithy.

Mold

Mold is in the north-eastern corner of Wales, close to the English border. It is nine miles north-east of Ruthin, over the Clwydian Hills, and ten miles west of Chester. Mold has a population of 9,568.

Market days
Wednesday and Saturday

Mold has been the county town of Flintshire since 1833. In the same year, the most spectacular item of craftsmanship in gold ever found in the UK – a Bronze Age ceremonial cape from about 1800BC – was discovered in a burial mound near the river Alyn. Made from more than half-a-kilogramme of gold, it must have belonged to someone of the highest status; it is now on display at the British Museum.

The name Mold may be a contraction of the Norman French name of Lord Robert de Montalt, named after his home region in Normandy, Mont-hault meaning high hill, who established a fortification here in 1093. The Welsh name, Yr Wyddgrug, suggests a hill or cairn, possibly used as a lookout. Control of the Norman motte-and-bailey settlement, the mound of which now gives wide views over the town, was seized on several occasions by the Princes of Gwynedd.

People have worshipped at the site of the parish church, St Mary the Virgin, since at least as far back as the thirteenth century. Enlargement during the late-fifteenth century was funded by Sir Thomas Stanley (Lord of Mold) and his second wife Margaret Beaufort, Countess of Richmond, in thanks for the victory of her son, Henry Tudor, at Bosworth Field. Later expansion, during the 1770s and between 1853 and 1873, gave us the impressive parish church that stands today.

Coal and lead ore were mined locally from the seventeenth century onwards, and the town prospered and grew. During the nineteenth century, it became established as an important administrative and judicial centre. The Assembly Hall overlooking the central crossroads became the focal point of the town when it was built in 1849. The Beatles played there at the beginning of the 1960s, on their way to world fame.

Mold's wide main street was built to provide plenty of space for livestock and produce, a decision for which today's market traders have good reason to be thankful.

CAMELLIAS
£10-00

St Mary's Church stands in a prominent position at the top of High Street. It contains a stained-glass window commemorating the landscape painter Richard Wilson – a founder member of the Royal Academy, who influenced both Turner and Constable, and is buried in the churchyard. Carved finials, ledges and water spouts around the exterior bear caricatures of animals and people – including Oliver Cromwell and David Lloyd George, opponents of the Anglican Church, who may be spotted among the gryphons and gargoyles above the main door.

The daily lives of the ordinary people of Mold were chronicled by Daniel Owen, the leading Welsh-language novelist of the late-nineteenth century and the town's most celebrated son. His father and two brothers died in a coal-mining accident when he was an infant. At the age of twelve, having received no formal education, he was apprenticed to local tailor Angel Jones, a Methodist chapel elder. The young Daniel discussed the topics of the day with customers and colleagues and acknowledged in later years that this provided 'a kind of college'. The tailor's shop where he worked is now the Pentan bar and restaurant, named after one of his short stories, Y Pentan – The Hob. His statue stands, fittingly, outside the library.

The former Cottage Hospital on Pwll Glas was built in 1877 in the Arts and Crafts style, its terracotta-and-white frontage imitating the stone-mullioned windows of a previous era. The wall around the house opposite, Tan y Coed, is decorated with stone heads believed to have come from the original tower of St Mary's Church. In medieval times, stone heads were added to buildings to guard against evil spirits.

The stock of Georgian and Victorian buildings in many a market town was built when households had servants that lived in, and kept horses that needed stables. These buildings are typically too large for today's needs and many have been converted into business premises or apartments. Impressive doorways, high ceilings and a sense of continuity with the past lend authority and dignity to the professionals – doctors, solicitors, accountants, architects and others – who tend to occupy them.

The
Jones
Partnership
SOLICITORS

01352 753388

Monmouth

Monmouth is fifteen miles north of Chepstow, at the other end of the famously scenic lower part of the Wye valley. The lands just across the Wye lie within Wales too; Offa's Dyke and the border with England are a couple of miles further east. Monmouth has a population of 8,877.

Market days
Friday and Saturday

Monmouth was once a walled town; this fortified gate tower, which guarded the Monnow Bridge, is the only one of its kind in the UK. It is certainly an impressive structure, though it is difficult to escape the conclusion that potential invaders could have waded across the shallow Monnow river elsewhere, to attack the town walls at a more vulnerable location.

The river Monnow flows into the Wye here, hence the name Mon-mouth. The confluence of the two rivers made the location accessible from three directions, along their valleys. From its origins as the Roman military town Blestium, the settlement grew into a centre of power under the Normans and eventually became a lordship of the Duchy of Lancaster.

The future King Henry V was born in Monmouth's thirteenth-century castle in 1387. The original structure has gone but it was replaced in 1673 by Great Castle House, built for the Duke of Beaufort and nowadays the headquarters of the Royal Monmouthshire Royal Engineers, the senior reserve regiment of the Territorial Army.

Under Henry VIII, following the Acts of Union, Monmouth became the county town of Monmouthshire. Curiously, in 1543, the second Act of Union placed the county under the Oxford judicial circuit, rather than the Welsh courts. It also conferred two Members of Parliament, rather than the usual (for Welsh counties) one. The notion that Monmouthshire somehow belonged more to England than to Wales (though it is manifestly west of Offa's Dyke and has many Welsh place names) persisted for centuries, even on maps and in official documents, until it was finally dispelled during the local-government reorganisation of 1974.

During the centuries that followed its elevation to county town, Monmouth acquired the prosperity, fine buildings and social cachet attendant to its status. The imposing Shire Hall was completed in 1724, in the style of Christopher Wren; it dominates Agincourt Square, named in commemoration of Henry V's famous victory.

The town is characterised today by its attractive range of shops, pubs and restaurants; interesting museums; fine Georgian and Victorian buildings; and a continuing air of prosperity, making it a great place to spend a few hours gently exploring.

From the elevated viewpoint of The Kymin, Monmouth's suitability as a market town is plain to see. It sits amid productive farmland – there's even a herd of cattle grazing in a field just beyond the town centre. It is accessible from all directions and provides good access to the central regions of both Wales and England. The continuing importance of the Wye Valley as a trading route is evident from the traffic thundering past on the A40, which runs between Pembrokeshire and Ross-on-Wye, linking to the M50 and M5 motorways.

Monmouth has many fine buildings – mainly from the eighteenth century in Monnow Street, seen here, and from the nineteenth century in Priory Street further up the hill. The wide main thoroughfare provided plenty of space for market stalls. There were once upwards of fifty taverns, a good number of which remain in business today. It can still be a very busy place – but then, that is the whole point!

Moco's
Mexican Restaurant
Moco's
Mexican Restaurant
All Day Breakfast
Lite Bites
Baguettes
Tortilla wraps
Nachos
ARTico

The larger shops are found on Monnow Street but there is also plenty to enjoy amongst the smaller retail premises in the lanes and courtyards around Agincourt Square. Church Street has numerous individual shops and cafés of character. Agincourt House, on the square itself, has a large selection of antique furniture and decorative items. Nicholas Frost Antiques, on Priory Street, specialises in figurines, Toby jugs and the China dogs found in so many Welsh parlours. Monmouth is a smart sort of place – even the dogs dress up to go shopping!

Agincourt House

"come inside & see for Yourself"

Garden Ornaments
Lighting
Bric-a-Brac
and much more

History is brought to life in Monmouth's two museums, both of which are close to Agincourt Square. The museum of the Royal Monmouthshire Royal Engineers is in Great Castle House. The New Market Hall, on Priory Street, is home to the Nelson Museum and Local History Centre. Some of the most important Nelson memorabilia in the UK may be seen here, thanks to a bequest in 1924 by Lady Llangattock, an avid collector and great admirer of the Admiral. Nelson visited Monmouth in 1802 and gave his blessing for the building of the Roundhouse, the white tower on top of The Kymin, now a National Trust property.

Below: Monmouth's most famous sons are commemorated at the Shire Hall. Henry V secured his victory at Agincourt with the decisive assistance of archers from this part of Wales. Charles Stewart Rolls was the son of Lord Llangattock, whose estate just west of Monmouth is now a golf course. Having studied engineering at Cambridge, Charles became an aviation and motoring pioneer, and co-founder of Rolls-Royce. In 1910, he became the first person to fly from England to France and back, non-stop. Tragically, he became Britain's first powered-flight fatality later that year, when his biplane (a model of which is in his hands here) crashed. The Shire Hall houses the courtroom where the Chartists were tried after their campaigns in Newport and also contains a tapestry showing Henry V addressing his troops at Agincourt.

Presteigne

Presteigne lies precisely on the Wales-England border, about twenty miles north-east of Builth Wells and slightly less than that from Ludlow. The narrow river Lugg forms the border; a couple of steps across the small stone bridge will take you from one country to the other. Presteigne has a population of 2,463.

Market day
Saturday

Situated in the Severn valley, where Wales bulges into Herefordshire and Shropshire, Presteigne grew in a perfect position for cross-border trade. Richard Haslam described it as "a lucky town, lying on an isthmus of land which links it with the wealthier and mellower east".

It was captured from the Welsh by the Mercian Saxons, which explains its location on the English side of Offa's Dyke. It had a weekly market in Tudor times and, from then until the mid-nineteenth century, held five annual fairs. Significantly, it was on the mailcoach route from London, Cheltenham and Gloucester to Aberystwyth, adding to its importance. From the sixteenth century onwards the County Assizes were held in Presteigne, and it eventually became the county town of Radnorshire. It lost this to booming Llandrindod Wells in 1884.

Presteigne is a small gem of a place, its architectural heritage largely intact. A feeling of tranquillity pervades the pleasant streets and the shaded greens of the church precincts. It was not always so: the town was attacked by Llywelyn ap Gruffudd in 1262; razed by Owain Glyndŵr in 1402; devastated by the plague in the fourteenth, sixteenth and seventeenth centuries; and laid waste by a catastrophic fire in 1681.

Nowadays, annual events include The Presteigne Festival of Music and the Arts at the end of August (respected for its promotion of contemporary music), the Sheep Festival (roots and world music, street theatre and comedy) and the 'Tour de Presteigne', the UK's largest rally for electric bicycles. Classic cars and motorcycles converge on the town in June and a vintage sports car rally and the Welsh Hill Climb follow in October.

The editor of Country Life magazine, Clive Aslet, wrote that he believed Presteigne to be one of Britain's top ten small towns.

The frontage of Radnor Buildings is decorated in ornate Arts and Crafts style; the carved timbers, detailed plasterwork – known as pargeting – and colourful mosaics combine to great effect. See also page 188.

The exotic-looking Assembly Rooms, built in Italianate style in 1869, overlook the crossroads at the centre of Presteigne. The tall Campanile is reminiscent of the towers of Osbourne House, Queen Victoria's home on the Isle of Wight. The arched arcades at ground level, now the town's public library, once housed market stalls. An elegant room on the upper level provides a pleasant venue for concerts, meetings and exhibitions.

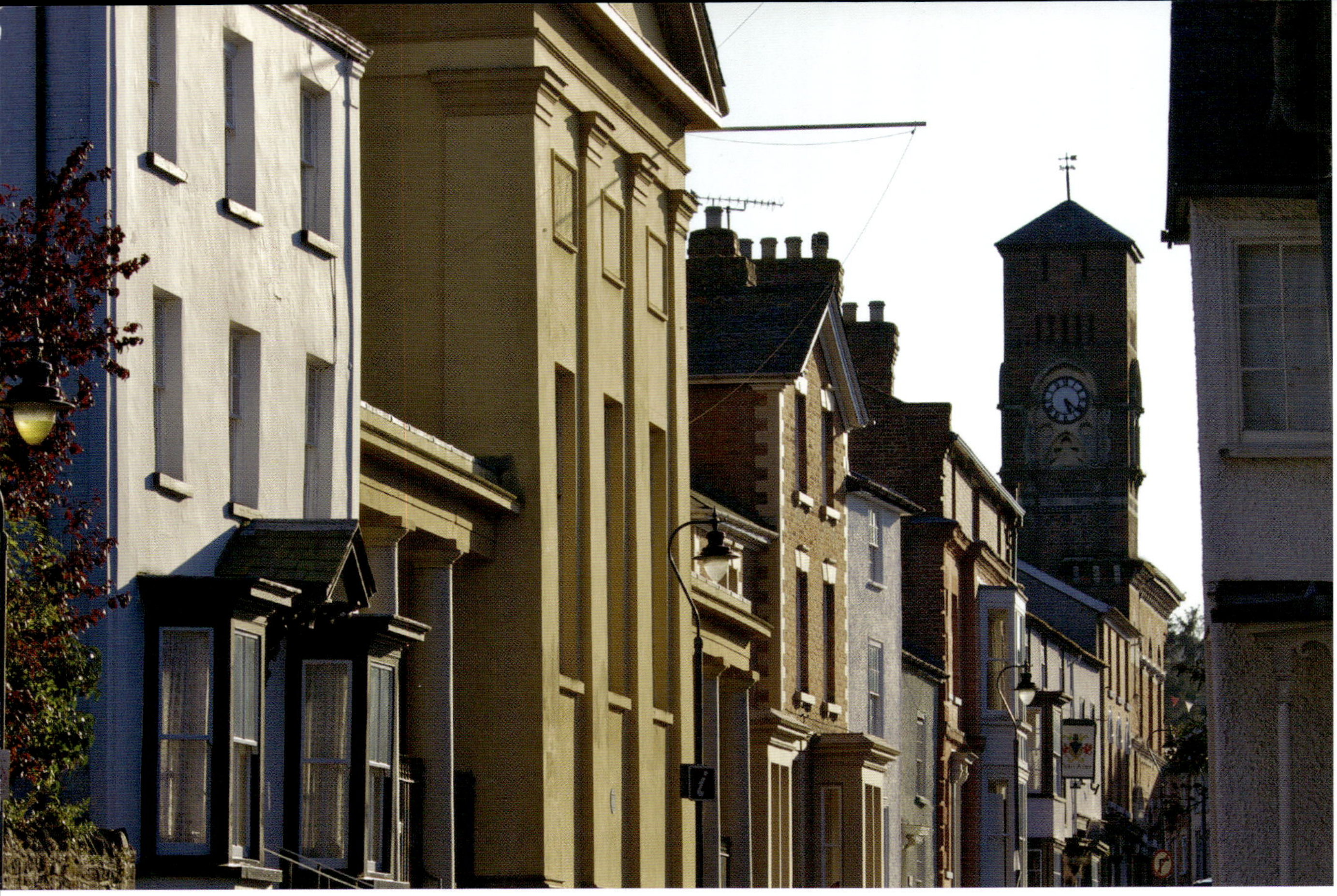

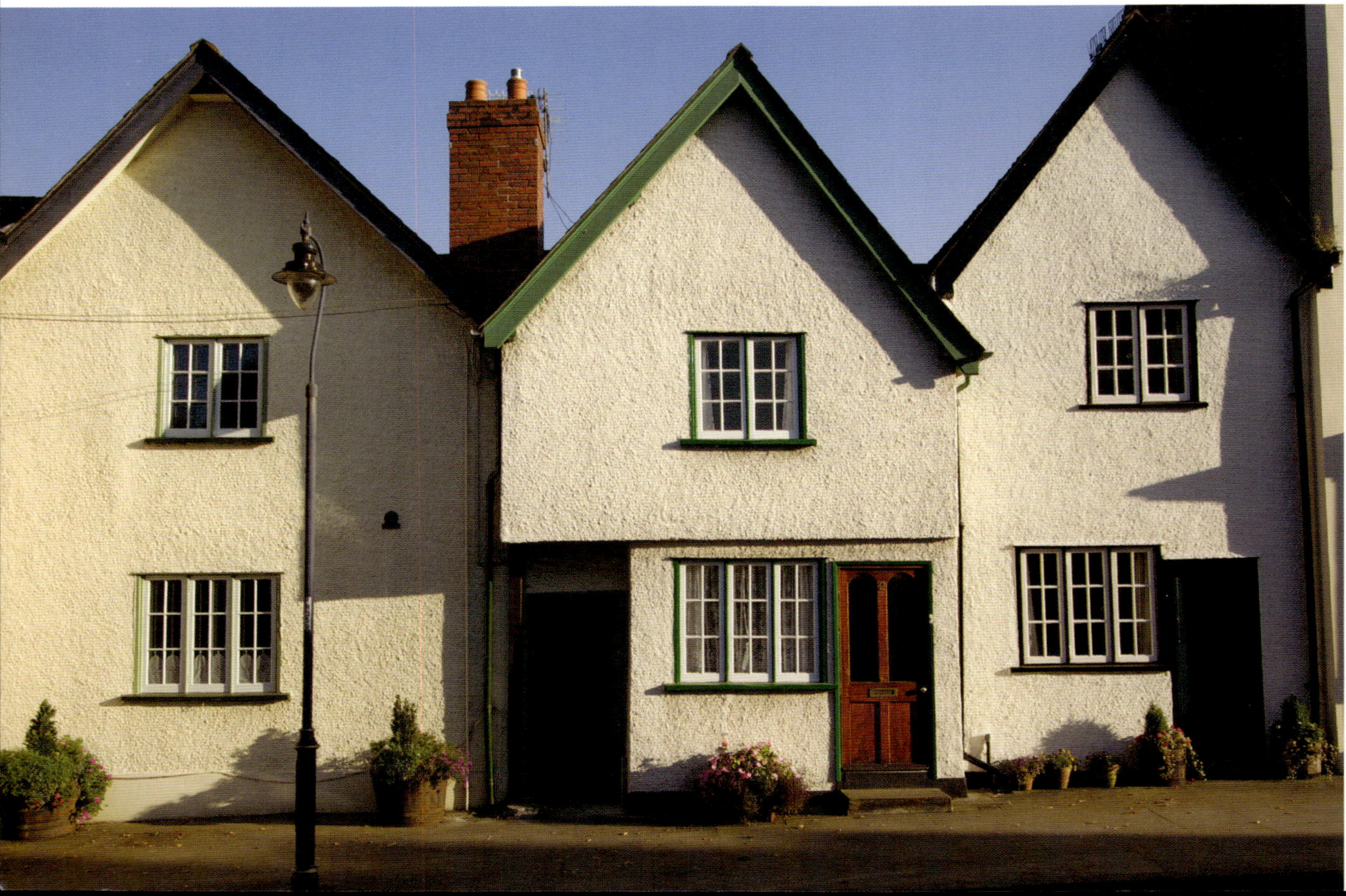

Opposite above: It isn't only geography that determines the location and success of a market town; it's also the consequent economic advantages. The population of Presteigne would barely half-fill the Royal Albert Hall, but look at the buildings the town could afford to build!

Above, left and opposite below: House names such as Tan House (the leather tannery), Garrison House and the Old Laundry reflect the origins of the buildings. Newell's Ironmongery Shop, on Broad Street, survived for more than two centuries from 1770 until 1974. The Museum of Welsh Life at St Fagan's, Cardiff, bought over 3,000 items of its unsold stock, much of it dating from the nineteenth century and in new condition.

SUNFLOWERS

Flowers by C

Above: The Judge's Lodging –
restored to its appearance in the
1870s – is a fascinating place to
explore the gaslit world of the
Victorian Judges, their servants
and their felonious clients.
Formerly the Shire Hall, the
building was completed in 1829 on
the site of the earlier County Gaol.

Right: The Radnorshire Arms
is a remarkable timber-framed
building – dated, over the front
door, to 1616. Originally a house, it
once belonged to Sir Christopher
Hatton, one of Elizabeth I's
courtiers. It became an inn in
1792, soon becoming the best-
known hostelry in the area, and
saw many social and political
gatherings during the following
centuries. The superb beams and
panels in the bar are from the
sixteenth century.

Pwllheli

Looking out over Cardigan Bay from the southern coast of the Llŷn peninsula, Pwllheli is fourteen miles west of Porthmadog and seventeen miles from Caernarfon. It is the terminus of the Cambrian Coast railway line from Machynlleth. Pwllheli has a population of 3,861.

Market days
Wednesday and Saturday

Rodney Adams Antiques has a tremendous stock of furniture, clocks, paintings and decorative items – and has staff with the skills to restore them properly. Nearby, one of Pwllheli's former chapels now serves as a large showroom for antique maps.

Pwllheli was already a small settlement in pre-Norman times under the Princes of Gwynedd; it was granted a charter as a borough by the Black Prince, in 1355. It grew over the centuries as the main town of the Llŷn peninsula, a position it maintains today. As sand dunes were stabilised, sea walls built and land reclaimed, so the centre of the town moved inland.

Since receiving its charter Pwllheli has held fairs and markets continuously. Hiring fairs, where farmhands would find employment, were held twice a year in May and November. The Eifionydd Agricultural Society set up its headquarters here in 1908 and numerous suppliers followed – including the Burgess company, suppliers of farm vehicles and machinery of all kinds up to and including tractors and combine harvesters.

The entrepreneur Solomon Andrews, of Cardiff, invested in Pwllheli at the beginning of the twentieth century, having visited briefly during a holiday in Llandudno. He established a horse-drawn tram service along the shore to Plas Glyn y Weddw, at nearby Llanbedrog, which he bought and opened to the public as an art gallery. The names of Solomon Bridge and Cardiff Road, and numerous buildings in a characteristic yellow brick, bear testimony to his influence on the town.

Pwllheli is a place where the Welsh language is strong (it is spoken by around eighty percent of the population) and you will hear it used as the natural medium of conversation around the streets and in the market, shops, cafés and pubs. Pwllheli has long been a hive of cultural and political activity through the Welsh language. David Lloyd George, from nearby Llanystumdwy, held meetings and gave speeches here. Plaid Cymru – The Party of Wales – was founded in what used to be the Maes Gwyn café (now a pet shop) just off the square.

Located on the coast of Cardigan Bay, Pwllheli once served as a small port and shipbuilding centre but, as this view at low water shows, the harbour dries out over much of its area and is limited in depth at the best of times. As ships became larger, and especially after the arrival of the railway in 1867, Pwllheli developed a combined role as a market town and seaside resort. In the distance is Hafan Pwllheli, a 400-berth marina owned by Gwynedd Council, which gives access to Cardigan Bay and the Irish Sea.

Opposite: Oriel Tonnau – the Sea Gallery – is a locally owned art gallery that takes the sea as its theme. Contemporary work, by numerous local artists, is displayed in a bright and pleasant exhibition space and there's a tea room at the back. The building was previously a paint shop and before that a woollen mill.

Above: Traditional Welsh rock has long been part of a day out at the seaside – either the colourful variety, with the name of the town running through it, or the brown 'number-eight' rock.

Left: The Penlan Fawr pub, dating from 1600, is the oldest building in Pwllheli. Its name shows that it once stood on the edge of the shore, before the sea defences were built. In 1836 around forty taverns were recorded in a street directory of the town.

Ruthin

Ruthin is in the upper part of the wide and fertile Vale of Clwyd, eight miles south-east of Denbigh and eleven miles north-east of Corwen – two other historic market towns that are more than worthy of a visit. Ruthin has a population of 5,218.

Market days
Produce Market (in Ruthin Gaol) last Saturday of each month, March to October and at Christmas

With the Clwydian Hills (an Area of Outstanding Natural Beauty) in the background, Ruthin looks the very model of a prosperous market town. St Peter's Church is evident to the left. The multi-dormered Myddelton Arms and the Castle Hotel (with four dormer windows along its roof) are just to its right.

Ruthin was controlled by Dafydd ap Gruffudd in the years leading up to Edward I's conquest of Wales in 1282. The Lordship of Ruthin was acquired by Reginald de Grey in 1284. He ordered the building of a castle and Ruthin was made a borough.

The town grew along narrow streets leading down from the castle to the river Clwyd. Many of the town-centre buildings built between the sixteenth and nineteenth centuries have survived to this day, there being very little flat land on which to build anything bigger. Much of Ruthin is now an architectural conservation area.

St Peter's Church has a spacious, double-naved layout and is distinguished by an especially fine carved-oak roof. It is unusual in having a collegiate close, a feature more typical of a cathedral. An Augustinian canonry is believed to have occupied the site before dissolution in 1536. Gabriel Goodman (1528-1601), Dean of Westminster for forty years, endowed the almshouses behind the church and also Ruthin Grammar School, which originally occupied a building nearby.

The need to house the agencies of law and order has given Ruthin a legacy of intriguing buildings. The timber-framed former courthouse of 1401, on the square, is now the National Westminster Bank. It was here in 1827 that Ruthin's medieval court documents were found, making this one of the best-documented towns in Wales. Between 1654 and 1916, thousands of prisoners – men, women and children; innocent and guilty – passed through the gates of Ruthin Gaol, on Clwyd Street, which is now open to all as a museum. The police station, built in 1891, and the former courthouse (now the library) may be seen on Record Street.

A sought-after place in which to live, and a rewarding place to visit and explore, Ruthin is undoubtedly one of the most attractive and fascinating market towns in Wales.

St Peter's Square occupies the hilltop and is rich in conservation-grade architecture. The backdrop of the surrounding countryside is visible down the streets that radiate from here. To reward those who made it up the hill, both a horse trough and a drinking fountain were considerately incorporated into the design of the town clock.

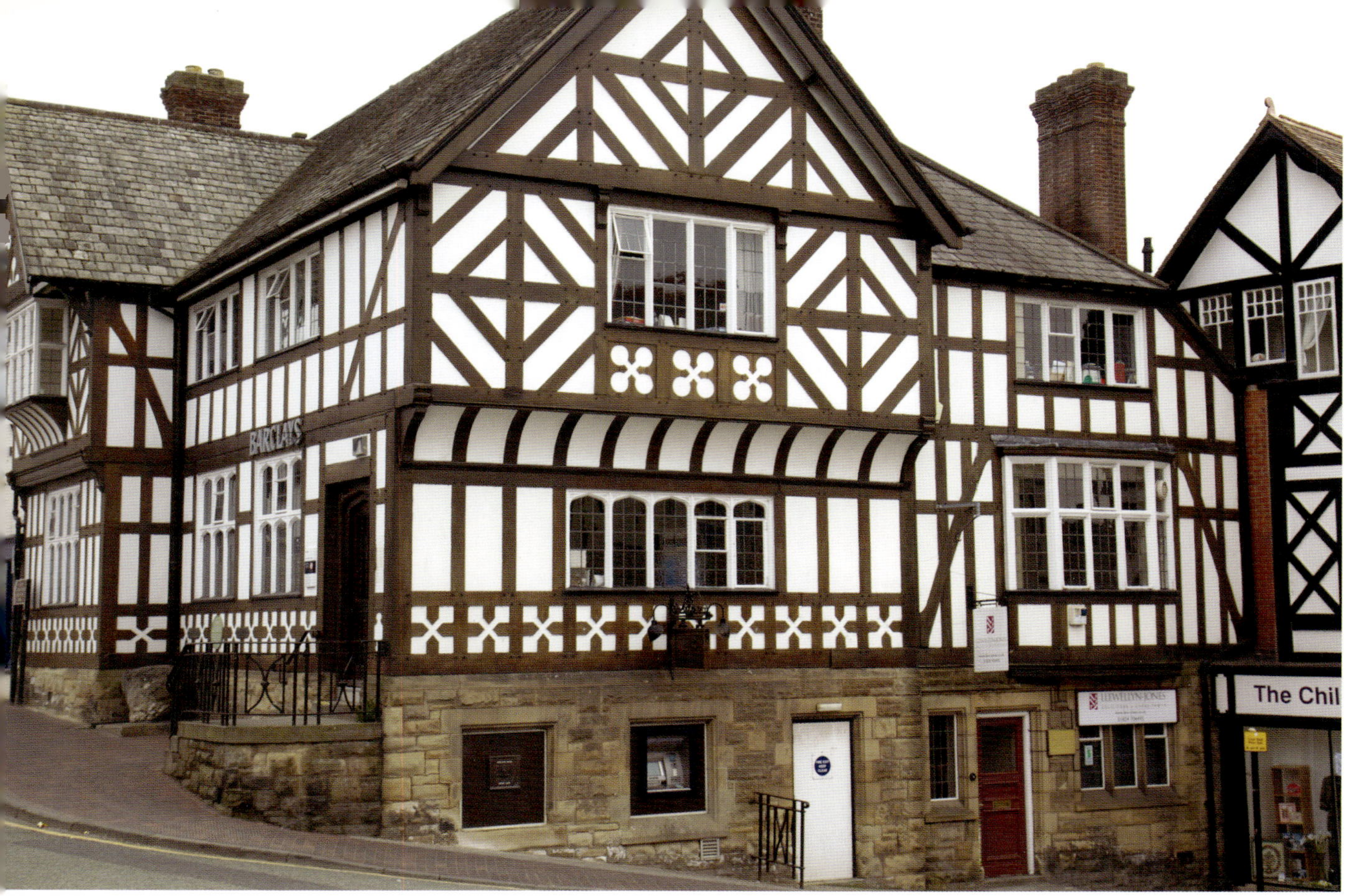
BARCLAYS
LLEWELLYN-JONES
The Chil

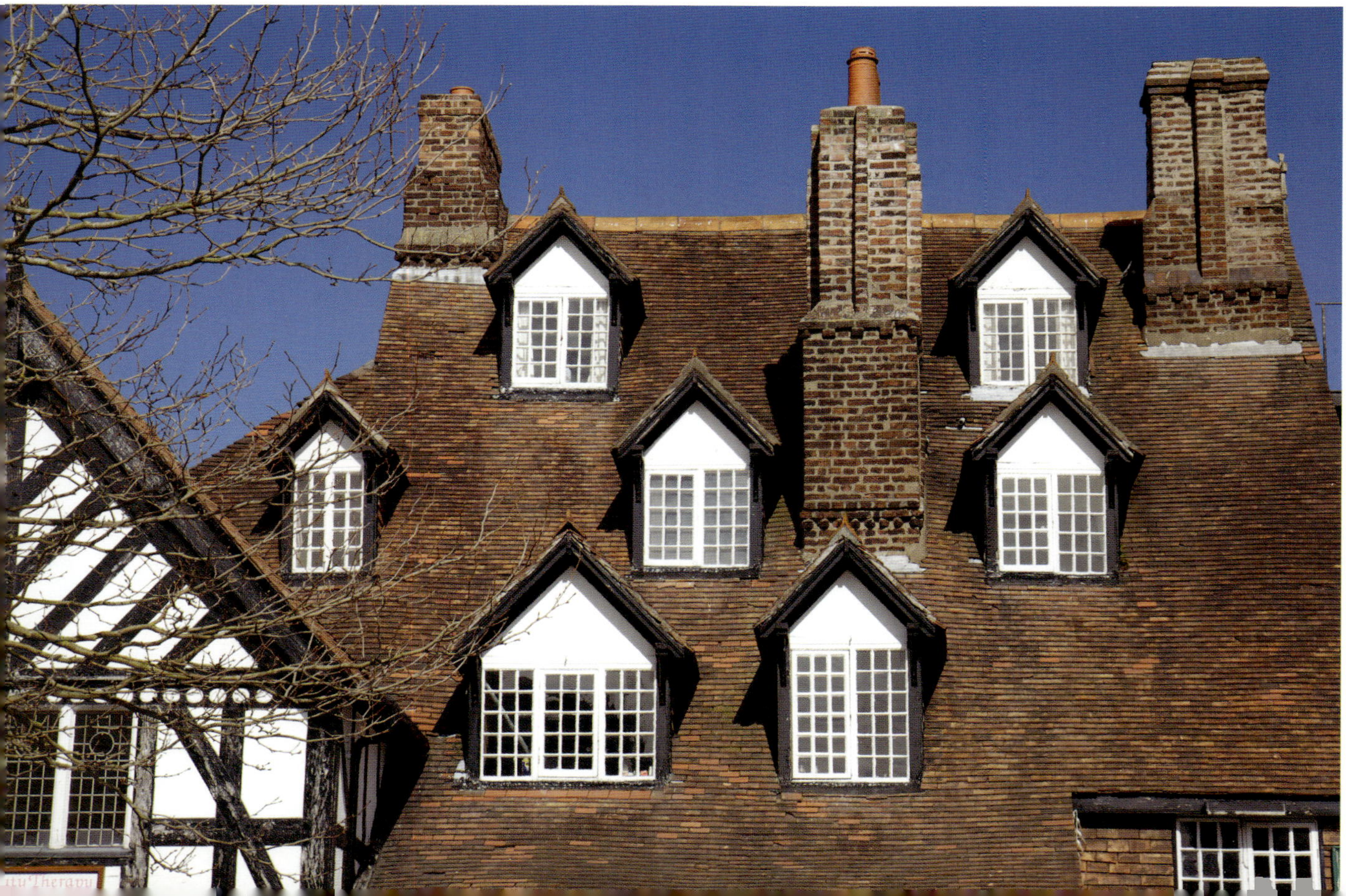

Ruthin has a wealth of black-and-white, timber-framed buildings of the sort that once graced every town of note in Wales. Three tiers of small dormer windows (The Seven Eyes of Ruthin) look out from the roof of the sixteenth-century Myddelton Arms. Banks, cafés and shops are housed in half-timbered buildings of enormous character.

Opposite: Ruthin Crafts Centre originally opened in 1982 and quickly established a strong reputation as one of Wales's premier centres for the applied arts. It has been rebuilt with upgraded workshops and exhibition spaces, and also houses a pleasant café and Ruthin's Tourist Information Centre. Ceramics sculptor Neil Dalrymple – seen here working on a head of Pan, the Greek god of shepherds – also makes a range of fish, bird and animal sculptures.

Left: Leonardo's Deli is a great place for home-made pies, sandwiches, preserves and all manner of tasty things.

Below: Produce markets are held regularly in the courtyard of Ruthin Gaol and in the market hall at the top of Market Street.

Nantclwyd y Dre, on Castle Street, is the oldest timber-framed town house in Wales. A rare survivor from around 1435, it would have been part of the rebuilding after Owain Glyndŵr burned the town to the ground in 1401 – yes, he was here too! The house was continuously occupied – by numerous families – for more than 500 years. It contains re-creations of seven ages of its history, with authentic furniture, fittings and decoration. A remote-controlled camera watches a colony of Lesser Horseshoe bats in the attic.

Usk

Usk is located midway between Newport and Abergavenny. The Usk is the longest river to run entirely within the borders of Wales. The town is a short distance along the A42 from the A449, which extends northward from J24 on the M4 motorway. Usk has a population of 2,318.

Market days
Farmers' Market first and third Saturday of each month

Location is everything; the ability to bridge the river here meant that livestock and produce could be brought to market from far and wide, by horse and cart, or by walking the animals, and conveyed onward to the customer.

To the Romans, this was Burrium – the location of a legionary fortress they built to control the local Silures, which was overtaken in importance by Caerleon from around AD75 onwards. Each subsequent wave of conflict in this tumultuous border region has left its mark. As with so many of the towns of lowland Wales, Usk was put properly on the map by the Normans; the Clare, Marshal and Mortimer families held sway here for several centuries, though the area was under Welsh control for a time during the mid-eleventh century.

The town grew around the present-day location of Twyn Square and in 1398 received its charter from Roger Mortimer, the local Marcher Earl. Owain Glyndŵr's rebellion brought great destruction to Usk; most of the buildings were razed in 1403. The Battle of Usk, fought at nearby Pwll Melyn in 1405, proved to be a turning point in the revolt, as Glyndŵr's forces were defeated by the local garrison. Adam of Usk, a cleric, lawyer and chronicler of Welsh history, recorded the story for posterity. He is commemorated by an inscription in Welsh, the first of its kind, on a brass plate in St Mary's Church.

Life went on relatively quietly here for several centuries, although Usk was captured by the Parliamentarians during the Civil War. The medieval layout remained largely intact. Industry arrived with the establishment of the Japanning Works in 1763 (japanning is the application of a durable black varnish, to metal or wood), and the town expanded towards the river. The prison was built in 1841; the addition of the Sessions House in 1887 made Usk the legal centre for the whole of Monmouthshire.

Today, Usk is well worth a visit to enjoy its riverside location and its pleasing buildings – and to explore the Usk Rural Life Museum. The town is also well known for the floral displays that deck its streets from springtime onwards, under the banner Usk in Bloom.

As we have seen, market towns stand at strategic points and serve a clearly defined region; Usk grew to serve the lower part of the river valley from which it takes its name. Though small in size, it has a remarkable number of attractive buildings and a fascinating history. This view is from Usk Castle, which stands on the site of an earlier Norman fortification built to guard the town.

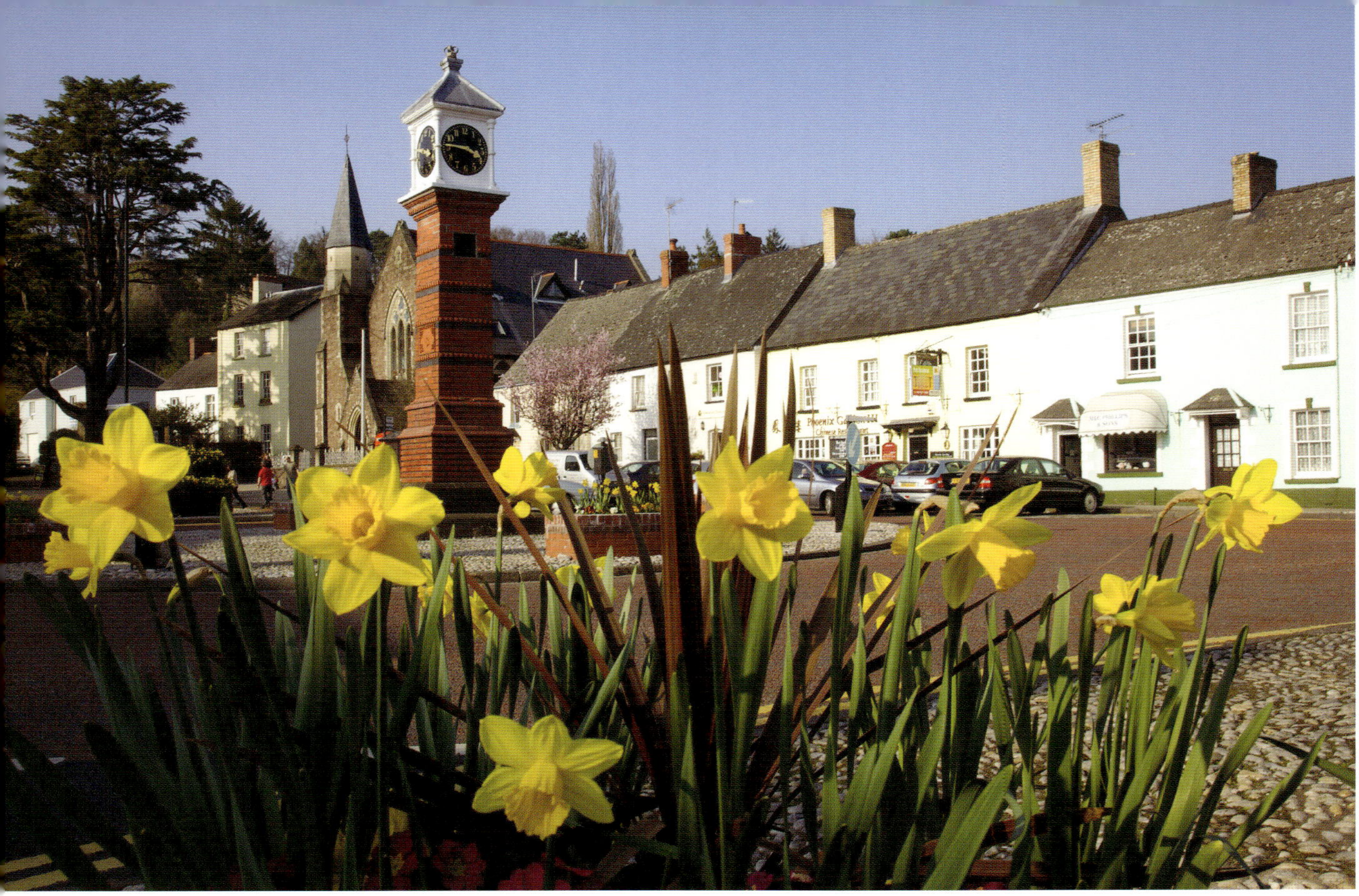

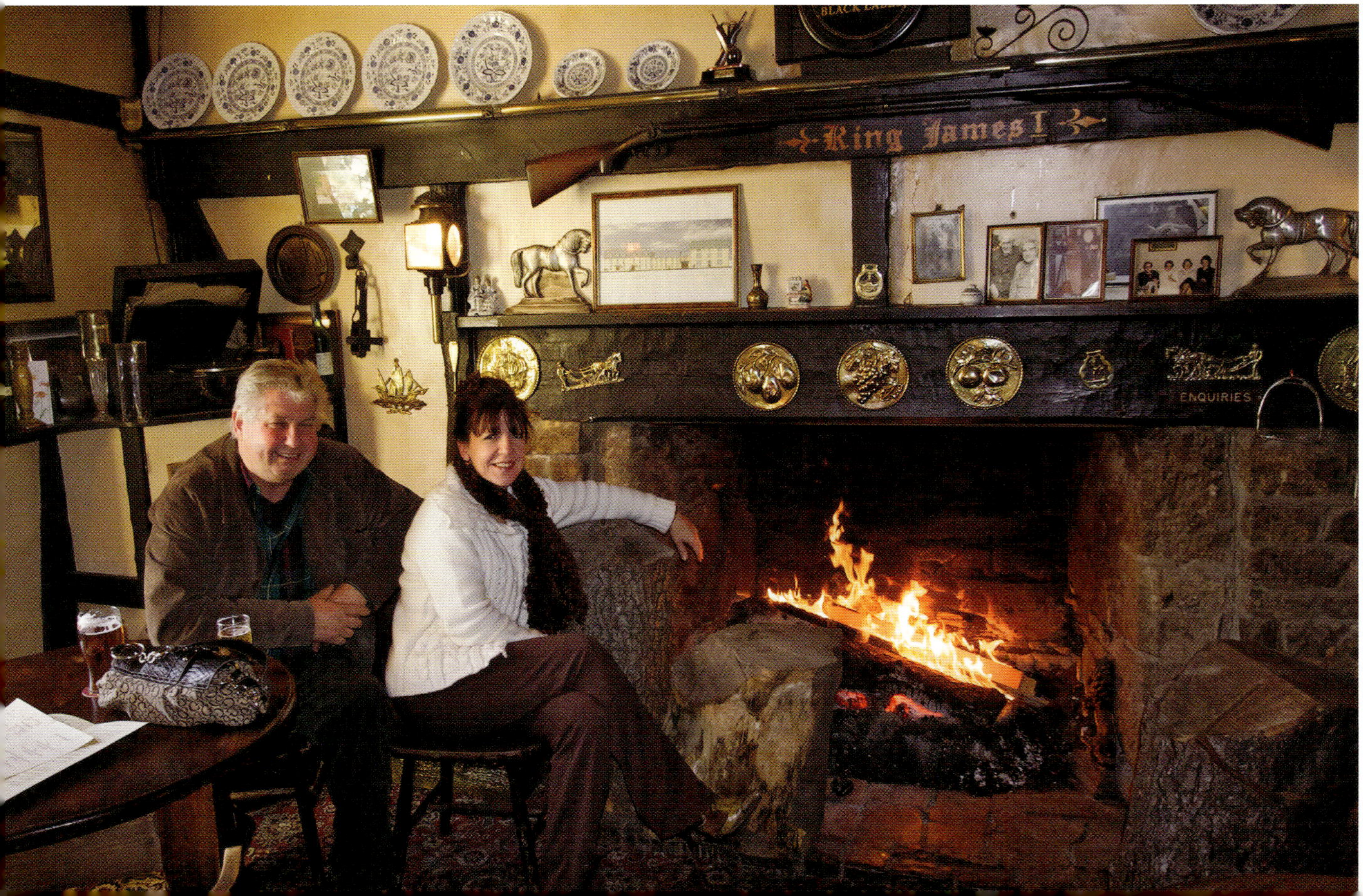
King James I
ENQUIRIES

Left: The appearance of rabbit pie, duck, partridge, guinea fowl and salmon on the menu of the Nag's Head illustrates the ready supply of traditional country food available in places such as Usk.

Below: Twyn Square hosts a produce market and there is also a regular indoor market in the community hall on Maryport Street.

Opposite above: The Town Clock, a prominent feature of Twyn Square, was built to commemorate Queen Victoria's Golden Jubilee in 1887.

Opposite below: The atmosphere of an authentic pub – this is the King's Head Hotel – just cannot be faked. The crackling log fire, the hint of woodsmoke, the local ales, good food and warm welcome bring a glow to the heart.

Above: The Usk Rural Life Museum, located in a fifteenth-century malt barn, portrays rural life in this part of Wales from Victorian times until 1945. It has displays of farm equipment and domestic items, along with reconstructions of a farmhouse kitchen, dairy and laundry; cobbler's and wheelwright's workshops; and superbly restored wagons and tractors. It is open from Easter until the end of October.

Right: St Mary's Priory Church was founded in the 1130s, as a Benedictine nunnery. It has a beautiful Tudor rood screen of remarkable quality, a fine organ and a rustic oak chest that once contained the parish records. It is the burial place of Wales's second Saint David, the seventeenth-century martyr Saint David Lewis.

Left: The timbered and crooked Old House, which stands on New Market Street, is indeed the oldest house in Usk. It is known to date in part from before 1550. The Usk Civic Society has prepared a Heritage Trail and printed guide (available from the Sessions House and local shops) that will lead you around many of the town's marvellous buildings.

Below: Jean Williams is one of Usk's best-known characters. She runs Sweet's fishing-tackle shop on Porthycarne Street and has customers all over the world who value her skills in tying imitation flies in a wide range of traditional patterns. Local fishermen know that if they find any interesting feathers, from a pheasant for example; these will be put to good use by Jean.

Welshpool

Twenty miles west of Shrewsbury, Welshpool is another town that looks to the uplands of Wales in one direction and the lowland shires of England in the other. A network of A-roads runs up and down the border and into central Wales. There's a main-line rail service and Montgomeryshire Mid Wales Airport is nearby. Welshpool has a population of 6,269.

Market days
Street market Monday;
Market Village (in Town Hall)
Monday to Saturday

When Montgomeryshire was created by Henry VIII's Act of Union in 1536, Welshpool (its largest settlement) became, in effect, the county town. Medieval Powis Castle was home of the Lords of Powys Wenwynwyn and later of the heirs of Robert Clive of India, whose collection of Asian treasures is on display and is a mile south of the town. The house and its magnificent terraced gardens are now under the stewardship of the National Trust and are open to the public.

Welshpool received its charter in 1241, from Gruffudd ap Gwenwynwyn, and became a Borough – under the name Burgus de Pola – in 1263. By the early-nineteenth century it was the sixth-largest town in Wales, enjoying prosperity from flannel making, brewing and tanning. Boats and barges were able to reach Pool Quay, the highest navigable point on the river Severn and a mile north of the town, carrying livestock, produce and all manner of goods to and fro. The Montgomeryshire Canal brought even better transport links and a stretch of it, passing through Welshpool, has been restored.

Welshpool has Wales's only cockpit remaining in its original location. It was in use until 1849, when cockfighting was made illegal, and is now the regional office of the Women's Institute. The livestock market grew into one of the largest in Europe; it has moved to state-of-the-art modern premises just outside town, the original site having been redeveloped as a supermarket.

Options for exploring the immediate area include the Offa's Dyke National Trail which passes just to the east, the Glyndŵr Way National Trail and The Welshpool and Llanfair Light Railway, which runs for eight miles along the Banwy Valley to Llanfair Caereinion, mainly at weekends between Easter and October.

The Town Hall was built in 1874 to replace a smaller structure, which the town's needs had outgrown. It houses a 'market village', with stalls selling food, clothing, antiques, CDs and gifts, which is open from Monday to Saturday.

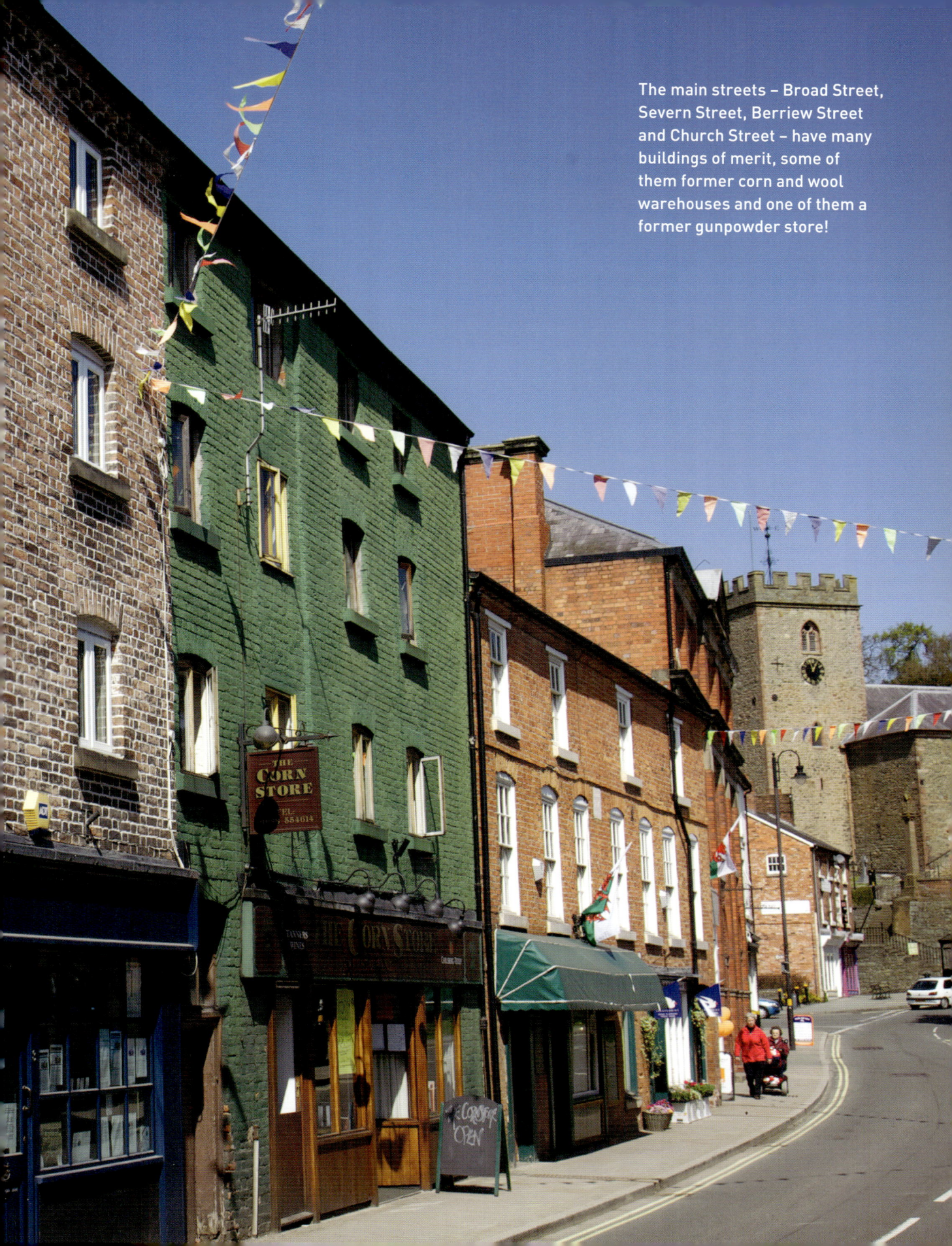

The main streets – Broad Street, Severn Street, Berriew Street and Church Street – have many buildings of merit, some of them former corn and wool warehouses and one of them a former gunpowder store!

Characterful details are to be found on many of Welshpool's buildings. The black-and-white half-timbered cottage was apparently given by a grateful Lord Nithsdale to Grace Evans, after she smuggled him out of the Tower of London in 1716.

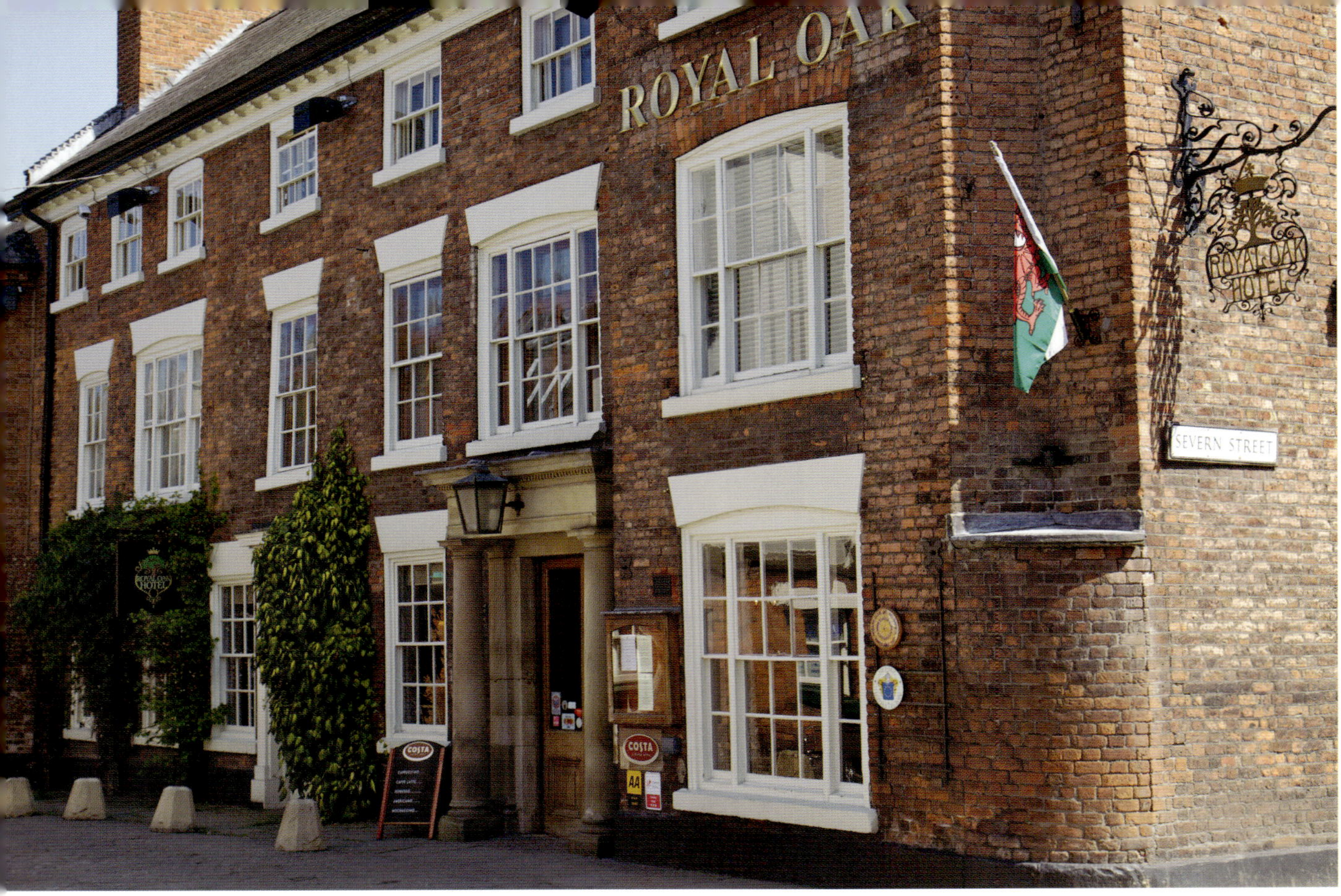
ROYAL OAK
ROYAL OAK HOTEL
SEVERN STREET
COSTA

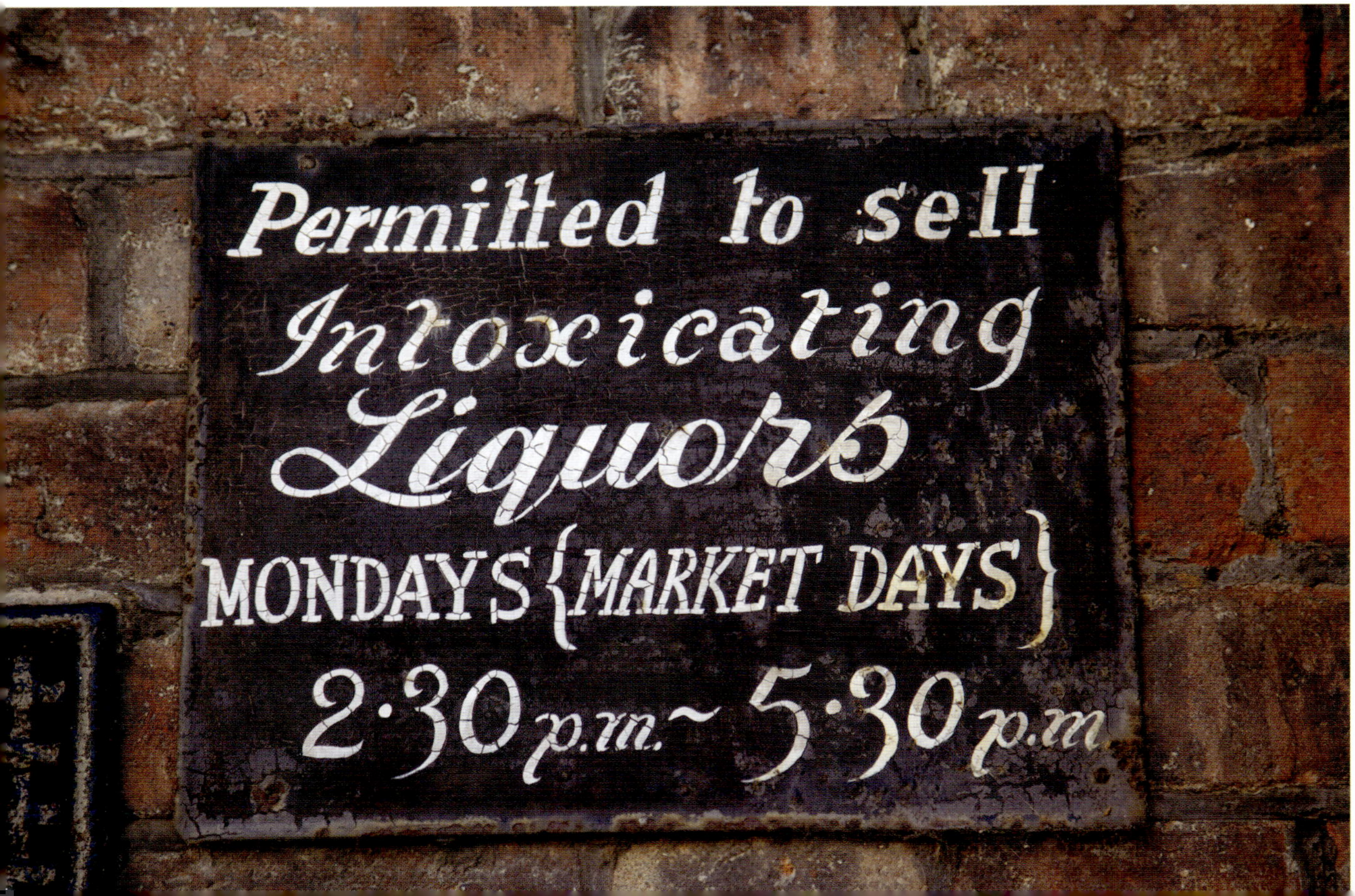
Permitted to sell
Intoxicating
Liquors
MONDAYS {MARKET DAYS}
2·30 p.m. ~ 5·30 p.m

Opposite: The Royal Oak Hotel acquired its royal connection when Queen Victoria visited Powis Castle. HM Queen Elizabeth II has also visited Welshpool in 2010. Stables behind the hotel accommodated the horses that drew the mail coaches. The main staircase – with its plain, narrow, square-section banisters and a handrail shaped to provide good grip – is in a style specific to Montgomeryshire.

Above and left: Powysland Museum. The canal towpath is a great place for a walk, with or without a four-legged friend. The Powysland Museum tells the story of the town and the canal; it is housed in one of thirty warehouses built along the canal during the nineteenth century.

Index

A

Aberaeron 103
Abergavenny 9
  Market Hall 11
Abergavenny Food Festival 11
Abergavenny Museum 15
Aberystwyth 135, 153, 183
Acts of Union 25, 153, 173
Adam of Usk 207
Agincourt 127
Agincourt House 179
Agincourt Square 173
Almshouses Museum 145
Alpha Presbyterian chapel 38
Ancaster Square 145
Angel Jones 168
Angel Vaults 45
Anglesey 127, 129, 131, 132
Aran Benllyn 17
Aran Fawddwy 17
Aran, river 77
Artbeat Brecon 28
Arts and Crafts style 169, 183
Assembly Rooms 185

B

Bailey Park 12
Bala 17
Bala Lake 17, 18, 21
Bala Lake Railway 21
Battle of Usk 207
Bawddwr, river 119
Bear Hotel 67, 68
Beaumaris 127
Bernard de Neufmarché 25
Betws-y-Coed 145
Bigod's Castle 103
Black Mountains 9, 67, 93
Black Prince 191
Black Sheep restaurant 91
Blaenau Ffestiniog 145
Blorenge 9
Boer War 41, 131
Books 93
Booth Hall 140
Brân, river 119
Brecon 9, 25, 26
Brecon Agricultural
  Society 25
Brecon Beacons 9, 25, 26, 67,
  93, 120
Bridge End Inn 67
Bristol Trader pub 87
Brychan 25
Brycheiniog 25
Bryn Mawr 81
Builth Wells 33
Burgess company 191

Burrium 207
Butter Market 101

C

Cadair Idris 77
Caerleon 207
Caernarfon 103, 191
Caersws 135
Caerwent 41
Cambrian Coast 153, 191
Cardigan Bay 191, 193
Carmarthen 41
Carmarthen Journal 47
Carmarthen School of Art 47
Carnival 39
Castle Hotel 197
Castle House 143
Cawdor Hotel 117
Cefni, river 127, 133
Centre for Alternative
  Technology 159
Ceredigion 103, 105, 109
Charles I 119, 161
Charles Stewart Rolls 181
Charles Stewart Vane-
  Tempest 157
Charles Tunnicliffe 132
Chartists 135, 181
Cheltenham 183
Chepstow 49, 101
Castle 56, 57
Chester 161, 163
Christmas Evans 127
Christopher Wren 173
Civil War 9, 56, 207
Clare family 207
Cleddau, river 87, 88
Clive Aslet 183
Clwydian Hills 163, 197
Clywedog, river 136
Constable 167
Conwy Castle 145
Corris 153, 159
Corwen 17, 197
Cottage Hospital 169
Country Life magazine 183
County Gaol 189
Court of Law 140
Cowbridge 59
  Old Wool Barn Arts and
  Crafts Centre 61
Cowbridge Food Festival 65
Cowbridge Grammar
  School 63
Cowbridge Physic Garden 63
Cow Inn 15
Crickhowell 67
Culidorus Stone 127

Cywain rural-heritage
  centre 22

D

Dafydd ap Gruffudd 197
Daniel Owen 168
David J Morgan 105
David Lloyd George 167, 191
Dean of Westminster 197
Denbigh 197
Derry Ormond Tower 105
Derwenlas 153
Dinefwr Castle 111
Dingle nature reserve
  127, 133
Dolau Cothi 103, 112
Dolgellau 17, 77, 153
Dragon hotel 71
Drovers Arms, The 45
Duchy of Lancaster 173
Duke of Ancaster 145
Dulais Brook 93
Dyfi, river 153
Dylife 153
Dynevor Family 111, 117

E

Edward I 33, 41, 111, 135,
  145, 197
Edward II 93
Eifionydd Agricultural
  Society 191
Eldon Square 81
Elizabeth I 189

F

Fair Trade town 67
Falcondale estate 103
Falcondale Hotel 107
Festival of Dance 39
Flintshire 163
Forest of Dean 49, 87
Forest Stewardship
  Council 143

G

Gabriel Goodman 197
Gaerwen Industrial Estate 127
Garrison House 187
Gasworks 82
George Borrow 119
George Prichard Rayner 131
Gerwyn Williams 125
Glamorgan Heritage Coast 59
Gloucester 183
Glyndŵr Way National Trail
  154, 215
Golden Lion Inn 25
Grace Evans 218

Great Castle House 173
Guildhall 41
Gwent 9, 49
Gwydderig, river 119
Gwydir Castle 145, 150
Gwynedd Council 193

H

Hafan Pwllheli 193
Haverfordwest 87
Hay Castle 93
Hay Festival of Literature 95
Hay-on-Wye 93
  Memorial Square 101
  Heads of the Valleys 9
Henry I 87
Henry III 93
Henry Tudor 67, 153, 161, 163
Henry V 127, 173, 181
Henry VII 127, 153
Henry VIII 150, 153, 173, 215
Hereford 9, 87, 93, 101
Herefordshire 93, 183
Honddu, river 25
House of Tudor 127
Howell Harris 38
Hywel the Good 67, 111

I

Industrial Revolution 9, 41, 77
Inigo Jones 148
Irfon valleys 33
Irish Sea 193
Ivybush Inn 42

J

Japanning Works 207
Jean Williams 213
Jen Jones Welsh Quilts
  Centre 107
John Elias 127
John Richard 145
John Wesley 117, 140
Judge's Lodging 189

K

Karl Showler 101
King's Head Hotel 211
Kington 25
Knighton 25

L

Lady Charlotte Guest 119
Lampeter 103
Lampeter Grammar
  School 103
Lampeter University 103, 107
Leonardo's Deli 203

Lion Street 31
Llanblethian 59
Llandeilo 111
   Newton House 111
Llandovery 103, 119
Llandovery College 120
Llandrindod Wells 183
Llandudno 131, 145, 191
Llanerchymedd 127
Llangefni 127
Llanidloes 135
Llanrwst 145
Llanthony Priory 93
Llanvihangel Crucorney 93
Llanystumdwy 191
Llyn Celyn 17
Llŷn peninsula 191
Llywelyn ap Gruffudd 33, 135, 145, 183
Llywelyn ap Iorwerth 93
Lord and Lady Llangattock 181
Lord Nithsdale 218
Lord Rhys 111
Lord Robert de Montalt 163
Ludlow 25, 183
Lugg, river 183

M

Mabinogion 119
Machynlleth 153
   Museum of Modern Art 153
   Spectrum Gallery 153
Maes Gwyn café 191
Malltraeth marsh 127
Mandalay Company 25
Marshal family 207
Mary Wynn 145
Maude de St Valery 93
Mawddach estuary 77
Meirionnydd 81, 82
Mercian Saxons 183
Methodism 17
Mold 163
Monmouth 173
   Local History Centre 181
   Nelson Museum 181
Monmouthshire 9, 173, 181, 207
Monnow Bridge 173
Mortimer family 207
Museum of Welsh Life, St Fagan's 187

N

Nag's Head 211
Nantclwyd y Dre 205
National Trust 111
National Westminster Bank 197
Neil Dalrymple 203
Newell's Ironmongery Shop 187

New Market Hall 181
Nicholas Frost Antiques 179

O

Ocky White's 91
Offa's Dyke National Trail 93, 215
Old House 213
Old Laundry 187
Old Quay 87
Oliver Cromwell 167
Oriel Tonnau 195
Oriel Ynys Môn 127, 132
Osbourne House 185
Owain Glyndŵr 67, 93, 111, 145, 153, 183, 205, 207
Owen de la Pole 153
Owen Tudor 127

P

Park Wells 33
Pembrokeshire 41, 87, 91, 175
Pembrokeshire Coast National Park 91
Penlan Fawr 195
Penllyn 17
Pentan bar and restaurant 168
Peterston Super Ely 65
Physicians of Myddfai 119
Plaid Cymru 191
Plas Glyn y Weddw 191
Plynlimon 93
Pont Steffan 103
Porthmadog 191
Portway 59
Powysland Museum 221
Presbyterian College 47
Preseli hills 91
Presteigne 183
   Sheep Festival 183
   Festival of Music and the Arts 183
Princes of Gwynedd 163, 191
Public Hall and Literary Institute 117
Pwllheli 191
Pwll Melyn 207

Q

Quaker Meeting House 91
Queen Charlotte 145
Queen Elizabeth Grammar School 47
Queen Victoria 185
Queen Victoria's Golden Jubilee 211

R

Radnor Buildings 183
Radnorshire 183
Radnorshire Arms 189
Regimental Museum of The Royal Welsh 25

Reginald de Grey 197
Reverend Thomas Charles 17
Rhodri Mawr 111
Rhys Prichard 119
Richard de Clare 59
Richard Haslam 183
Richard Wilson 167
Riverside Market 89
Riverside Shopping Centre 89
Rodney Adams Antiques 191
Roger Mortimer 207
Rolls-Royce 181
Ross-on-Wye 175
Roundhouse 181
Royal House 161
Royal Monmouthshire Royal Engineers 181
Royal Welsh Show 33, 37
Royal Welsh Winter Fair 37
Ruthin 163, 197, 201, 203
Ruthin Crafts Centre 203

S

Saint David 212
Saint David Lewis 212
Saint Teilo 111
Sea Gallery 195
Sessions House 207
Severn, river 136
Severn valley 140, 183
Shire Hall 91, 173, 181, 189
Shire Horse Show 12
Shropshire 183
Silures 207
Simon de Montfort 93
Sir Anthony Hopkins 63
Sir Christopher Hatton 189
Sir Grimbald Pauncefoot 67
Sir Kyffin Williams 132
Sir Richard Evans 67
Sir Robert Taylor 41
Sir Thomas Stanley 163
Sir William Nott 42
Skirrid 9
Smallholder and Garden Festival 37
Snowdonia 17, 84, 153
Solomon Andrews 191
Solomon Bridge 191
South Gate 59
St Cyngar's Church 127
St David's College 103
Stephen's Castle 103
St Grwst Church 146
St Idloes 135
St John the Evangelist 30
St Mary's Church 167, 169
St Mary's Priory Church 15, 212
St Mary the Virgin Church 163
St Peter's Church 103, 197
St Peter's Square 199
Sugar Loaf 9

T

Tancred 87
Tan House 187
Thaw, river 59
The Beatles 163
The Seven Eyes of Ruthin 201
Thomas Edward Ellis 22
Thomas Telford 145
T H Roberts 82
Timbuktu 93
Tomen y Bala 21
Tonn Press 119
Tools for Self Reliance 75
Top Town Traders 87
Tour de Presteigne 183
Tower of London 218
Traeth Bychan 131
Trewythen Arms 139
Trinity College 47
Tryweryn, river 17
Turner 77, 167
Twyn Square 207
Ty Hwnt i'r Bont 148
Tŷ Meirion 81
Tywi, river 111, 119
Tywi valley 111, 112, 119

U

University of Wales 47
Upper House Farm 75
Usk 207
   Castle 209
   Civic Society 213
   Prison 207
   Rural Life Museum 207, 212
Usk, river 25

V

Vale of Clwyd 197
Vale of Glamorgan 59
Vaughan family 15
Viscount Castlereagh 157

W

War memorial 39, 41, 107, 131
Welsh Hill Climb 183
Welshman's Candle 119
Welshpool 215
White Hart Inn 71
White Lion Royal Hotel 22
Wild Fig 65
William de Breos 9, 93
William Owen 88, 91
William Teulon 117
William the Conqueror 25
William Williams 119
Wnion, river 79
Worcester 25
Working Men's Institute 140
Wye, river 49, 51, 93, 101
Wye Valley 49, 93, 175
Wye Valley Walk, The 93

Latest titles published by Graffeg

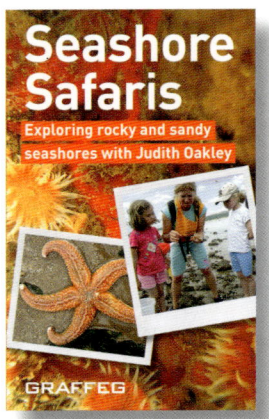

Seashore Safaris
Judith Oakley
978 1 905582 33 4
£9.99

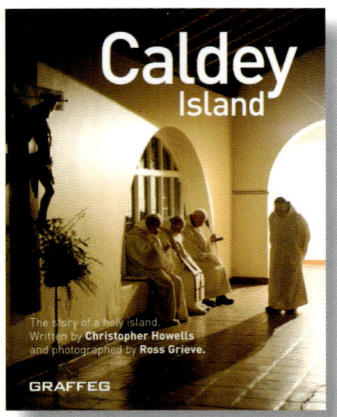

Caldey Island
Christopher Howells and
Ross Grieve
978 1 905582 14 3
£14.99

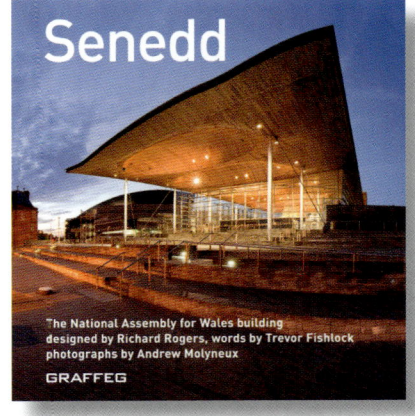

Senedd
Trevor Fishlock and
Andrew Molyneux
978 1 905582 43 3 (English)
979 1 905582 44 0 (Welsh)
£18.99

Other Graffeg titles

About Cardiff
David Williams
ISBN 978 09544334 2 0 £12.95

About Mid Wales
David Williams
ISBN 978 1 905582 05 1 £6.99

About North Wales
David Williams
ISBN 978 1 905582 04 4 £6.99

About South East Wales
David Williams
ISBN 978 1 905582 07 5 £6.99

About South West Wales
David Williams
ISBN 978 1 905582 06 8 £6.99

About Wales
David Williams
ISBN 978 0 9544334 7 5 £14.99

Bryan Webb's Kitchen
Bryan Webb
(H/b) ISBN 978 1 905582 32 7 £20.00
(P/b) ISBN 978 1905582 22 8 £14.99

Celtic Cuisine
Gilli Davies
ISBN 978 1 905582 10 5 £14.99

Coastline Wales
Andy Davies
ISBN 9781905582167 £25

Discovering Welsh Gardens
Stephen Anderton, Charles Hawes
ISBN 9781905582204 £18.99

Discovering Welsh Houses
Michael Davies
ISBN 9781905582136 £14.99

Food Wales – a second helping
Colin Pressdee
ISBN 978 1 905582 15 0 £14.99

Food Wales – eating out guide
Colin Pressdee
ISBN 978 1 905582 11 2 £7.99

Landscape Wales
David Williams
(H/b) ISBN 9780954433413 £24.95
(P/b) ISBN 9780954433437 £12.95

Pembrokeshire
David Wilson
ISBN 9781905582358 £25

Skomer
Jane Matthews
ISBN 978 1 905582 08 2 £14.99

Village Wales
David Williams
ISBN 978 1 905582 03 7 £14.99

Welsh National Opera
Caroline Leech
ISBN 9781905582006   £14.99

www.graffeg.com

GRAFFEG